GARLIC

First published in the United States in 2000 by Periplus Editions (HK) Ltd., with editorial offices at 153 Milk Street, Boston, Massachusetts 02109 and 5 Little Road #08-01, Singapore 536983.

Created by Co & Bear Productions (UK) Ltd.

Copyright © 2000 Co & Bear Productions (UK) Ltd.

Photographs copyright © 1999 Andy Cameron.

All rights reserved. No part of this publication may be reproduced or utilized in any form or by any means, electronic or mechanical, including photocopying, recording, or by any information storage and retrieval system, without prior written permission from Periplus Editions.

Library of Congress Cataloging-in-Publication Data is available.
ISBN: 962-593-941-5

DISTRIBUTED BY

USA	CANADA	JAPAN	SOUTHEAST ASIA
Tuttle Publishing	Raincoast Books	Tuttle Publishing	Berkeley Books Pte. Ltd
Distribution Center	8680 Cambie Street	RK Building, 2nd floor	5 Little Road #08-01
Airport Industrial Park	Vancouver, British Columbia	2-13-10 Shimo-Meguro, Meguro-ku	Singapore 536983
364 Innovation Drive	V6P 6M9	Tokyo 153-0064	Tel: (65) 280-3320
North Clarendon, VT 05759	Tel: (604) 323-7100	Tel: (03) 5437-0171	Fax: (65) 280-6290
Tel: (802) 773-8930	Fax: (604) 323-2600	Fax: (03) 5437-0755	
Tel: (800) 526-2778			

First edition
06 05 04 03 02 01 00   10 9 8 7 6 5 4 3 2 1
Printed and bound in Italy

GARLIC RECIPES BY LEADING CHEFS FROM AROUND THE WORLD

GARLIC

photographed by Andy Cameron

PERIPLUS

6		The taste of garlic
10		**Soups**
24		**Appetizers & snacks**
40		**Vegetable dishes**
56		**Pasta & rice**
76		**Fish & seafood**
116		**Poultry & meats**
153		Glossary
154		Contributors
158		Index

The taste of garlic

Garlic is one of a very few culinary ingredients that inspires both love and loathing. It adds a distinctive flavor and aroma to food, and is believed to have numerous medicinal qualities, ranging from purifying the blood to curing a cold. However diverse its characteristics, the one factor that has made garlic fall in and out of favor over the ages is that the flavor that makes it so delicious also has an odorous effect on the breath!

Probably originating in the wild in southwestern Siberia, garlic (*Allium sativum*) is one of the oldest cultivated plants. A perennial, it is easy to grow. The name derives from *gar*, which means "spear" — it has spear like leaves when it is growing — and *lic* or *leac*, which means "leek." It is the most powerfully flavored member of the onion family. The familiar bulb is divided into many fat cloves, each covered with papery white or pink skin. The leaves are flat, grayish green in color, and grow about 12 in (30 cm) high. In late summer, the small lily like pink or white flowers are grouped in protruding round heads.

There are many different kinds of garlic, which vary in size, shape, taste, pungency, cloves per bulb, and color. Botanists classify all true garlics in two groups: the original *Ophioscorodon* (Ophios), or hard-necked, and the cultivated *Sativum*, or soft-necked. Specimens of the former tend to be more colorful and have fewer but larger cloves per bulb than *the* latter. They include the Purple Stripe garlics with their white, thick bulb wrappers, which are usually strongly flavored, particularly the Metechi variety. However, Siberian Purple Stripe garlic is very mild. These are beautiful garlics and they store well. Another group belonging to the this category is the Porcelain garlics. Their bulb wrappers tend to be white and thick like parchment and as you peel away the clove wrappers, they are often striped with purple. The cloves themselves are few and fat, and tend to be strong tasting. Rocambole garlics often have thinner bulb wrappers than other hard-necked varieties and lots of purple striping and blotching. They are more difficult to grow, require a cooler climate, and do not keep well. Although they have few cloves, they are renowned for their delicious flavor.

Artichoke garlics (*Sativums*) are more commonly seen. California Early and California Late are among the easiest to cultivate. They have an abundance of cloves, are generally large, and store well. Their flavor and color vary, depending on the variety. Whereas Simoneti and Red Toch have a mild flavor, Chinese Purple and Purple Cauldron are pungent and strongly flavored. Silverskin garlics are usually twisted into braids, as they keep well and have long necks. The skins are white, although the clove wrappers can be very pink. They have more cloves per bulb, but their bulb size is smaller than the artichoke garlics. Their flavor is usually strong and pungent. Creole garlics are an exception within the silverskin group. Their skins and wrappers are rose pink, and they are among the best garlics to eat raw, as they have little heat.

Not all the plants that we think of as garlic are actually garlic. For instance, elephant garlic (*Allium ampeloprasum*) is a leek. It is milder in flavor, more oniony with a distinct aftertaste, much larger in bulb size, and its leaves resemble leeks. Ramsons (*Allium ursinum*) is a broad-leaved wild garlic found in European woodlands. It has a distinctive acrid flavor and aroma that hangs heavily in the air on a warm day. Garlic chives (*Allium tuberosom*) grow like chives and have hardy, flat leaves. They have a pleasant, mild garlic flavor, which makes them ideal in salads.

On a nutritional level, garlic is rich in minerals, especially sulfur (sulphur), which gives it its renowned pungency, and, as the oil is excreted through the lungs, makes the breath smell. It also contains calcium, phosphorus, and iron in smaller amounts, and is rich in vitamins B1 and C. Garlic's health-giving properties are being researched, but we know that it has molecules that are antifungal, antiseptic, and anti-thrombotic (prevents blood clotting), and it also possesses properties to aid digestion.

Available all year round, garlic is plentiful and cheap in the summer and autumn. In early summer, you can find fresh garlic, which is more difficult to peel but has a less concentrated flavor. As the weeks go by, it begins to dry out, and in early winter, prices go up. In spring, before the new season's harvest is available, care should be taken when choosing bulbs, as the contents can dry out completely, leaving empty husks. Look for large, clean, firm bulbs with dry, unbroken skins. Store garlic in a terracotta pot, wire basket, or vegetable rack, and keep in a cool, dry place where the air can circulate. Refrigeration affects the flavor and dehydrates the cloves. Ready-dried garlic should keep for up to two months in ideal conditions.

Garlic has an infinite variety of uses in the kitchen: a squeeze of juice will flavor a salad dressing or a whole bulb can be added to a simmering, rich stew. A small amount will enhance other flavors, while a large amount, used fresh, will make your mouth tingle. Getting the quantity right is a personal decision. The general rule is to allow the flavor to complement other ingredients rather than dominate them. How you prepare garlic is the real secret of flavor release. If you peel the papery skin away without damaging the clove inside, no oils are released. The more you cut garlic, the stronger the flavor develops. Whole garlic cloves can be used to "temper" oil or melted butter at the beginning of a recipe, and then discarded, leaving behind a trace of flavor. Cooking time also affects the strength of flavor. The longer you cook garlic, the less it will taste and smell, and the more creamy the flavor will become. For the merest suggestion of flavor, use a milder variety, keep the cloves whole or cut into thick slices, and add at the beginning of cooking. For a bold, powerful flavor, finely chop or crush the cloves and add toward the end of cooking.

To prepare garlic, the cloves can be crushed with the skin on, or blended whole, and then the skin removed in due course. Peeling individual cloves can be difficult if the paper is wrapped tightly, but soaking them in water for an hour before you want to use them allows you to ease off the papery skin without damaging the clove. Cloves can be crushed by putting them under the flat blade of a large kitchen knife or cleaver and banging with your fist; or by placing them, concave-side down, on a plate with a pinch of salt and firmly pressing with the ball of your thumb.

Soups

12 | Potato & goat cheese soup with garlic leaves

15 | Baked garlic soup with a poached egg

16 | Corn soup

18 | Roasted red bell pepper & garlic soup with goat cheese & garlic toast

21 | Roasted garlic & bread soup

22 | White garlic soup with langoustines & almond-infused mushrooms

Potato & goat cheese soup with garlic leaves

Ingredients | *serves 4*

- 6 medium (2 lb/1 kg) baking potatoes
- 4 oz (125 g) leeks
- 4 oz (125 g) onions
- 6 tbsp (3 oz/90 g) butter
- 14 garlic leaves (green tops of young garlic)
- 3¾ cups (1½ pints/900 ml) vegetable stock
- 3 tbsp crème fraîche
- 4 oz (125 g) fresh goat cheese, finely diced
- salt and freshly ground black pepper

1| Peel and dice the potatoes into 2 in (5 cm) pieces.

2| Remove the outer leaves from the leeks and trim them; rinse and dice into 2 in (5 cm) pieces. Peel and dice the onions into 2 in (5 cm) pieces.

3| In a large, heavy saucepan, melt the butter and fry the leeks and onions together until softened but without color, about 5 minutes.

4| Add 10 of the garlic leaves and the potatoes to the mixture, then stir in the stock. Season to taste with salt and pepper.

5| Let simmer until the potatoes are tender, about 3 minutes. Let cool and blend to a purée. If the mixture appears to be too thick, gradually add extra stock and transfer to a clean pan. Return to the heat and let simmer, stirring occasionally.

6| Season and stir in the crème fraîche. The soup should now be the same thickness as heavy (double) cream. Reheat slowly, stirring the soup occasionally.

7| To serve, place some goat cheese in the bottom of each soup bowl and pour over the very hot soup. Float a garlic leaf on top of each bowl of soup and serve immediately.

Note_Garlic leaves – flat and slender leaves from the garlic plant – are relatively expensive due to being seasonal and will only be available from a good quality greengrocer.

Baked garlic soup with a poached egg

1 | Preheat oven to 400°F (200°C/Gas Mark 6). Meanwhile, split the bulbs of garlic open and separate into cloves. Do not peel them but remove the papery outer husks.

2 | Lay the garlic cloves and bread in a deep ovenproof dish or casserole, drizzle with olive oil, and season generously. Place in the center of the oven and bake until the bread cubes are golden and crisp, about 15 minutes.

3 | During this time, heat the stock with the bay leaf to a simmer in a large, heavy saucepan. When the garlic and bread are ready, pour over enough stock just to cover the solids. Drizzle with some more oil, cover with foil, and return to the oven for 1 hour. After 10 minutes, reduce the heat to 325°F (160°C/Gas Mark 3).

4 | When done, remove the soup carefully from the oven and let cool for 30 minutes. Remove the bay leaf and purée in a food processor, then pass through a coarse sieve. Refrigerate, covered, until needed.

5 | To serve, preheat oven to 475°F (240°C/Gas Mark 9). In a large heavy saucepan, reheat the soup to tasting temperature (i.e., not boiling nor lukewarm). Check the seasoning and ladle into ovenproof bowls. Crack and place an egg in the center of each bowl. Film with yet more oil and bake for 5 minutes, or until bubbling round the edges. Serve the soup in the same bowls but warn your guests that it will be extremely hot.

Note_ Do not try and make this marvelous Spanish soup with old dry garlic. Only new season's garlic—the very moist, thinly skinned type available in late spring and early summer—will do. It is sometimes referred to as "wet garlic."

Ingredients | serves 6

_ 4 new season's garlic bulbs (see note)
_ 1 baguette (or other good white bread), cut into cubes
_ olive oil for drizzling
_ about 6 1/4 cups (2 1/2 pints/ 1.5 litres) chicken, beef, or vegetable stock, or water
_ 1 bay leaf
_ 6 medium eggs
_ salt and freshly ground black pepper

Corn soup

Ingredients | *serves 4*

- *6 tbsp (3 oz/90 g) butter*
- *6 tbsp (3 oz/90 g) finely chopped garlic*
- *1 cup (4 oz/125 g) finely chopped onions*
- *4 cups (1 1/4 lb/600 g) corn kernels (stripped from the cob)*
- *2 cups (16 fl oz/500 ml) water*
- *7 tbsp (3 1/2 fl oz/100 ml) heavy (double) cream*
- *4 slices garlic butter (see below), to serve*
- *salt and freshly ground black pepper*

for the garlic butter
- *11 tbsp (5 1/2 oz/160 g) butter*
- *4 tsp finely chopped garlic*
- *juice of 1 lemon*
- *4 oz (125 g) flat-leaf parsley, freshly picked (if possible) and finely chopped*

1 | To make the garlic butter, soften the butter in a food processor with the garlic, lemon juice, and a pinch of salt. When the mixture is well combined, stir in the parsley.

2 | Cover the garlic butter in plastic wrap and roll into a cylinder. Let set in the refrigerator until the soup is ready to serve.

3 | To make the soup, first melt the butter in a large, heavy saucepan over medium heat.

4 | Add the garlic and onions. Reduce the heat and fry slowly until translucent, about 5 minutes.

5 | Add the corn, cover with the water, and let simmer until the corn is soft, about 20 minutes.

6 | Transfer the mixture to a blender or food processor. Add the cream and season to taste. Purée for about 3 minutes until smooth. Strain through a fine sieve to remove any remaining fibrous corn skins.

7 | To serve, pour the soup into individual bowls. Serve immediately with a slice of garlic butter floating on top of each one.

Note _ The garlic butter enriches the soup and intensifies its earthy flavor. It is also good served with fish.

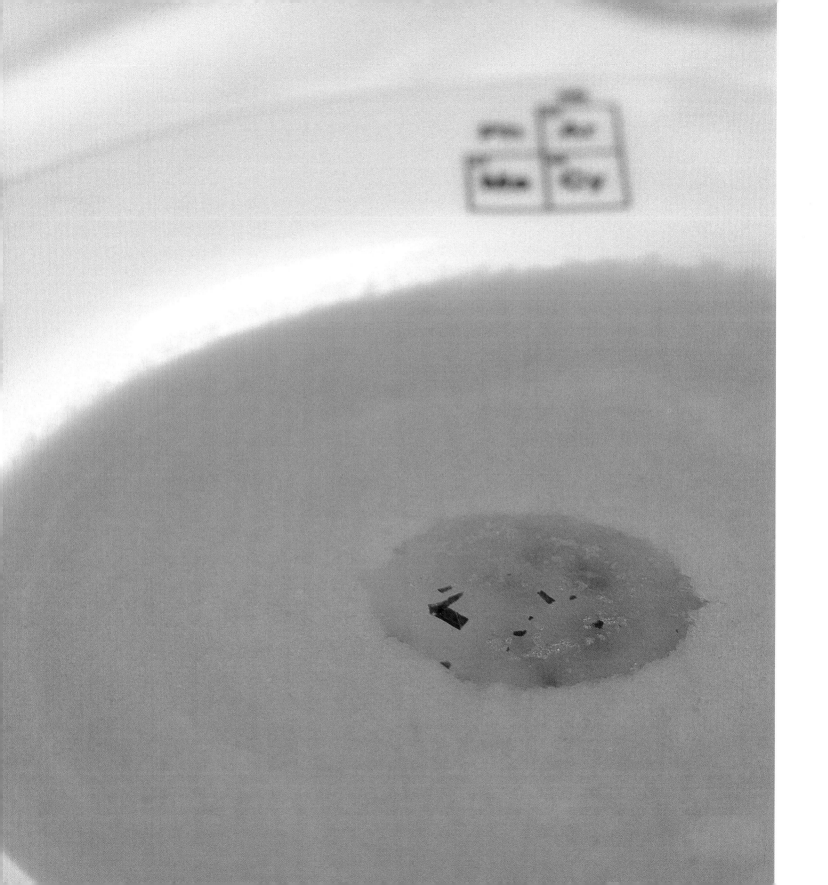

Roasted red bell pepper & garlic soup with goat cheese & garlic toast

Ingredients | serves 4

- 4–5 medium red bell peppers (capsicums), stems removed, halved, and seeded
- 10 garlic cloves, peeled
- 2 cups (16floz/500ml) water
- 4 tbsp olive oil
- 1 tbsp balsamic vinegar
- salt and freshly ground black pepper

for the garnish
- 4oz (125g) fresh goat cheese
- ½ tbsp finely chopped chives
- ½ tbsp finely chopped parsley

for the garlic toast
- 2 garlic cloves, cut in half across the middle
- 4–8 slices bread (ciabatta, baguette, or other good-quality bread, preferably a day old)
- 2 tbsp extra virgin olive oil

1 | Preheat oven to 350°F (180°C/Gas Mark 4). Meanwhile, roughly chop the peppers (capsicums) and place in a large, deep roasting pan or ovenproof dish with the garlic cloves, water, olive oil, and balsamic vinegar. Season and bake until slightly charred and soft, about 30 minutes.

2 | While the soup ingredients are cooking, prepare the garnish and garlic toast. Crumble the goat cheese, chop the herbs, slice the garlic cloves in half, and cut the bread. When the peppers (capsicums) are ready, transfer to a blender or food processor and process until smooth and creamy. Check the seasoning, reheat the soup in a large, heavy saucepan, and keep warm.

3 | Toast the bread, then rub with the cut garlic cloves and drizzle over the oil.

4 | To serve, pour the soup into serving bowls. Sprinkle some crumbled goat cheese and herbs into the center of each bowl and serve with garlic toast.

Note _ This recipe is delicious hot or cold. Quantities are for four generous servings or six appetizers.

Roasted garlic & bread soup

1 Preheat oven to 275°F (140°C/Gas Mark 1). Remove the crusts from the bread and roughly break it into large chunks.

2 Peel the garlic bulbs, divide into cloves, and peel each one. Place them on a baking sheet with the bread. Liberally douse with olive oil and sprinkle with thyme. Bake until the garlic cloves are soft, brown, and roasted, 15–20 minutes.

3 Pour the milk and stock into a large, heavy saucepan, stir, and bring to a boil. Remove from the heat and add the baked bread and garlic to the mixture to moisten them.

4 Roughly purée the soup and season with salt and pepper to taste.

5 To serve, divide the soup among 4 bowls and add a drizzle of olive oil to each one just before serving.

Ingredients | *serves 4*

- 1 large crusty loaf of bread
- 4 garlic bulbs
- extra virgin olive oil to taste
- 1–2 tbsp thyme, freshly picked (if possible)
- 1 cup (8floz/250ml) milk
- 3 3/4 cups (1 1/2 pints/900ml) chicken stock
- salt and freshly ground black pepper

White garlic soup with langoustines & almond-infused mushrooms

Ingredients | serves 6

- 8 garlic cloves, peeled
- 1 cup (5oz/150g) blanched almonds
- 6¼ cups (2½ pints/1.5 liters) fish stock
- 2 tsp extra virgin olive oil
- 2 tbsp sherry vinegar
- 5 tbsp finely chopped chervil, freshly picked (if possible)
- salt and freshly ground black pepper

for the garnish

- olive oil for frying
- 6 langoustine tails (see note), blanched, then shells removed (ask your fishmonger to do this for you)
- 6 porcini (ceps)
- 5 tbsp extra virgin olive oil
- 1 tbsp sherry vinegar
- 2 tbsp finely shredded fresh mint, freshly picked (if possible)
- ⅓ cup (2oz/60g) blanched almonds

1 | To make the soup, first blanch the garlic in a large, heavy saucepan of boiling water. Repeat this procedure 7 times in fresh batches of boiling water.

2 | In the bowl of a food processor or blender, place the almonds, blanched garlic, and fish stock. Blend to a nice silky purée. Stir in the extra virgin olive oil, sherry vinegar, and chervil, then adjust the seasoning. Transfer to a large saucepan or bowl.

3 | Blend the soup in the saucepan or bowl once more, this time using a hand blender. Cover and let chill in the refrigerator for at least 2 hours.

4 | To prepare the garnish, heat 1 large, heavy frying pan and, when hot, add some olive oil. Pan-fry the langoustine tails and porcini separately until golden, about 2–3 minutes. Remove from the pan and let cool.

5 | To serve, divide the chilled soup among 6 serving bowls. Garnish with extra virgin olive oil and sherry vinegar. Top with the langoustines and porcini and sprinkle with the mint and almonds. Serve immediately.

Note_Langoustines are small, spiny lobsters found in European waters. Large shrimp (prawns) may be substituted.

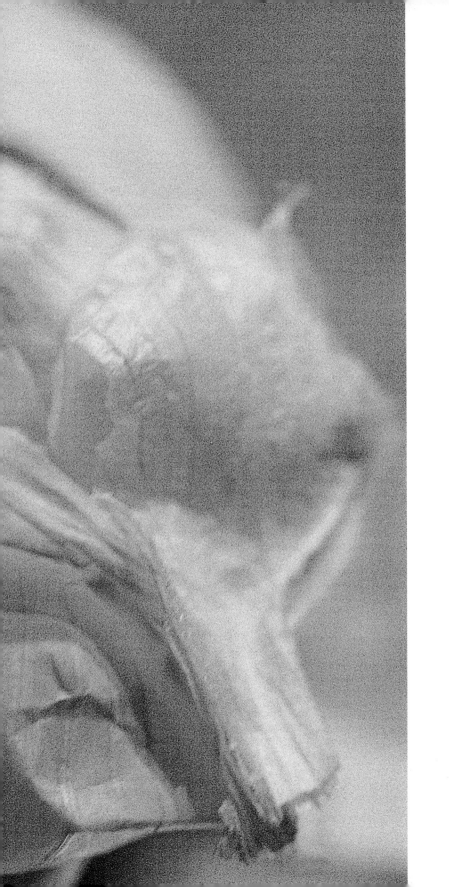

Appetizers & snacks

27 | Bagna cauda

28 | Grilled eggplants with garlic & anchovy dip

31 | Crudités with pesto of garlic, chervil & fennel

32 | Pan-Asian oysters Rockefeller

35 | Roast new season's garlic with homemade cheese

36 | Alioli

38 | Pan amb tomat

Bagna cauda

1| Place the garlic, milk, and butter in a medium, heavy saucepan and let simmer over low heat, stirring occasionally, until the garlic is soft and most of the milk has been absorbed, about 20 minutes.

2| Remove the pan from the heat and mash up the softened garlic with a fork. Add the anchovies and then mash them together with the garlic.

3| Return the pan to the stove over low heat and slowly add the olive oil to create an emulsion, stirring constantly. Then stir in the chopped walnuts. When the oil has been absorbed, after 2–3 minutes, the dip is ready for serving.

4| To serve, transfer the dip to a fondue-style pot or other heated dish so that the dip can be kept warm throughout the meal. Arrange the vegetable crudités and crusty bread on plates around the dip.

Note_ Bagna cauda, a classic dish from Piedmont in northern Italy, translates as "hot bath," as the dip is kept warm over a candle flame. The vegetables and bread are traditionally dipped into the warm bagna cauda and eaten straightaway. You should fillet and rinse the salted anchovies before adding them to the saucepan.

Ingredients | *serves 4–6*

_ 4 garlic bulbs, cloves separated and peeled
_ 1 1/4 cups (1/2 pint/300 ml) milk
_ 1 cup (8oz/250g) butter, diced
_ 7oz (200g) good-quality salted anchovies
_ 1 3/4 cups (14 fl oz/400 ml) extra virgin olive oil
_ 4 walnuts, shelled and coarsely chopped
_ selection of sliced or chunked mixed vegetables to include: celery, fennel, scallions (spring onions), bell peppers (capsicums), cucumbers, and radishes
_ crusty white bread, sliced

Grilled eggplants with garlic & anchovy dip

Ingredients | serves 4

- 2 large firm eggplants (aubergines), thinly sliced
- olive oil for brushing
- salt and freshly ground black pepper

for the dip

- 1 garlic bulb, cloves separated
- 1 cup (8 fl oz/250 ml) milk
- 10 anchovy fillets in oil, drained
- handful flat-leaf parsley sprigs, leaves picked and finely chopped
- 4 tbsp olive oil
- juice of 1 lemon

1| To make the dip, place the garlic cloves, still in their skins, in a small, heavy saucepan and cover with water. Bring to a boil. Remove from heat, drain, and run under cold water until the garlic is cool enough to peel.

2| Place the peeled garlic in the milk in a small, heavy saucepan and let simmer for 30 minutes. Let cool, then drain, reserving the milk. Using a mortar and pestle (or in a bowl), mash the garlic with the anchovies. Stir in the parsley, olive oil, and lemon juice. Add just enough of the reserved milk to make a slightly runny purée. Set aside but do not refrigerate.

3| Lay the eggplant slices on a baking sheet, brush with olive oil, and season with salt and pepper. Turn the slices over and then repeat the oiling and seasoning process.

4| Heat a barbecue, a stove-to-grill pan, or an oven broiler (grill) to very hot. Broil (grill) the eggplants until brown and crispy, about 6–8 minutes, turning halfway through. Be careful not to overcrowd the broiler (grill) and, if necessary, cook in 2 or more batches. As the slices are cooked, let cool and pat with paper towels to remove excess oil.

5| To serve, arrange the crispy eggplant slices on a large platter accompanied by a bowl of the dip.

Crudités with pesto of garlic, chervil & fennel

1 | To make the pesto dip, cut the garlic cloves in half; remove the inside green shoot from each one. Blanch 7 times in fresh batches of boiling water; set aside.

2 | Wash, trim, and chop the fennel. Place in a large, heavy saucepan, together with the spices, Pernod, and blanched garlic. Cook slowly until the Pernod is reduced by two-thirds, then transfer to a food processor.

3 | Add the olive oil; blend and then adjust the seasoning. Transfer to a serving bowl and scatter with the chervil. Cover and refrigerate while you prepare the vegetables.

4 | Wash and trim the vegetables, then cut into small pieces of about 2 bites each.

5 | To serve, place the dip in the center of a large serving platter. Arrange the vegetables around the bowl, chop the mint finely, and sprinkle over the vegetables. Serve immediately.

Ingredients | *serves 12*

_ 1 bunch each: Treviso radicchio, baby scallions (spring onions), celery hearts, radishes with tops, baby carrots, baby turnips, asparagus, and mint, freshly picked (if possible)
_ 2 red and 3 yellow bell peppers (capsicums)
_ 3 heads of chicory (endives)
_ 12 baby zucchini (courgettes)
_ 1 romaine lettuce heart
_ 4oz (125g) cherry tomatoes
_ 4 violet artichokes (available from any good Italian vegetable supplier)

for the pesto dip

_ 7oz (200g) garlic cloves, peeled
_ 7oz (200g) fennel
_ 1 star anise
_ 2 tsp cardamom seeds
_ 1/4 cup (2floz/60ml) Pernod
_ 2/3 cup (1/4 pint/150ml) extra virgin olive oil
_ 1 tbsp finely chopped chervil
_ salt and freshly ground black pepper

Pan-Asian oysters Rockefeller

Ingredients | serves 4

- 6 tbsp (3 oz/90g) butter
- 2 tbsp finely diced smoked bacon, rinds removed
- 2 tbsp minced shallots
- 8 oz (250g) fresh spinach
- 16 oysters, shelled (reserve the liquor and shells for serving)
- 2 cups (16 fl oz/500ml) Coconut Cream (see below)
- ½ tbsp Herb Topping (see below)
- ½ cup (2oz/60g) scallions (spring onions), minced
- 4 tsp tobiko caviar (available from Asian stores)

for the herb topping

- 1½ cups (125g/4oz) panko flakes (Japanese bread crumbs, available from Asian stores)
- ½ cup (2oz/60g) grated Parmesan cheese
- 1 tbsp mixed dried herbs (thyme, dill, basil, tarragon)
- ¼ cup (2 fl oz/60ml) olive oil
- 1 tbsp finely chopped garlic

for the coconut cream

- 1 tbsp butter
- 1 tbsp all-purpose (plain) flour
- ⅛ tsp Madras curry powder
- 1 star anise
- ½ tbsp brown sugar
- 3 tbsp Pernod
- reserved oyster liquor (see above)
- ½ cup (4 fl oz/125ml) clam juice (from 2-3 cherrystone clams)
- 1 cup (8 fl oz/250ml) coconut milk
- 1 tsp lemon juice
- salt and ground black pepper

1 | To make the herb topping, mix all the ingredients together in a bowl. Cover with plastic wrap and chill for 30 minutes.

2 | For the coconut cream, place a large, heavy saucepan over medium heat and melt the butter in it. Add the flour and stir to form a roux. Next, add the curry powder, star anise, and brown sugar; continue to stir, about 3 minutes.

3 | Now stir in the Pernod, reserved liquor from the oysters, clam juice, and coconut milk. Bring the mixture to a boil, whisking constantly to avoid separating out the coconut milk. Lower the heat and let simmer for 15 minutes, stirring occasionally. Stir in the lemon juice and season to taste. Keep warm.

4 | To cook the oysters, preheat oven to 425°F (220°C/Gas Mark 7). Meanwhile, heat a large, heavy frying pan and sauté the bacon in the butter briefly until lightly browned, about 5 minutes.

5 Add the shallots and spinach to the pan and cook until just wilted, about 2 minutes. Transfer the mixture to an ovenproof dish and add the oysters. Cover with coconut cream and bake for 3–4 minutes until bubbling. Meanwhile, preheat the broiler (grill).

6 Transfer the spinach and baked oysters to the reserved shells. Sprinkle with herb topping and brown under a hot broiler (grill) until golden brown, about $1^{1}/_{2}$ minutes. Meanwhile, quickly mix together the scallions and caviar in a bowl.

7 To serve, divide the shells among 4 plates, garnish with the caviar mixture, and serve immediately. Alternatively, serve the oysters on a bed of couscous, garnished with fresh herbs.

Note_ If you prefer, have your fishmonger remove the oysters from the shells, but remember to reserve the liquor and shells to serve.

Roast new season's garlic with homemade cheese

1 To make the cheese, line a fine sieve with a large piece of clean cheesecloth (muslin), or similar coarsely woven cloth and place it over a deep bowl. Tip the yogurt into the cloth and fold it over to cover the yogurt. Place a 2 lb (1kg) weight on top of the bundle and then refrigerate overnight. The next day, the yogurt will have separated in two; the whey will have drained into the bowl, leaving the curd, now the cream cheese, wrapped in the cloth.

2 Transfer the cheese to a bowl and mix the parsley through. Season to taste and refrigerate until needed.

3 To roast the garlic, preheat oven to 325°F (160°C/Gas Mark 3). Peel away the loose outer layer of skin from the garlic bulbs and carefully slice away the top quarter from each bulb. Season the cut sides and brush with olive oil. Place the bulbs in an ovenproof dish and replace the tops to resemble small lids. Brush the outside of the bulbs with oil and place in the oven. Roast for 1 hour.

4 Remove the dish from the oven and carefully lift out the bulbs, placing one on each of 4 plates. Tip the lids to one side and place spoonfuls of cheese on the exposed garlic cloves. Serve with teaspoons so that diners can scoop away all the succulent garlic flesh. The remaining cheese can be served with fine olive oil and crusty bread.

Note_This is an adaptation of a recipe by Alice Waters, whose restaurant, Chez Panisse in California, is famous for, among other things, staging a garlic festival. This dish only works with moist, very fresh new season's garlic bulbs. As the cheese is homemade, you must prepare it a day in advance so it can stand in the refrigerator overnight. Any cheese you don't use can be kept, covered, in the refrigerator for 1 week. Put the garlic in the oven to roast 1 hour before you plan to eat.

Ingredients | serves 4

_ 2 lb (1 kg) unsweetened plain yogurt, preferably organic
_ small bunch flat-leaf parsley, freshly picked (if possible) and coarsely chopped
_ 4 new season's garlic bulbs
_ extra virgin olive oil for brushing
_ good olive oil and crusty bread, to serve
_ salt and freshly ground black pepper

Alioli

Ingredients | *serves 6–8*

_ 2 whole eggs and 2 egg yolks
_ 8 garlic cloves, peeled and crushed
_ 1¼ cups (½ pint/300ml) vegetable oil
_ 1¼ cups (½ pint/300ml) olive oil
_ juice of ½ lemon (optional)
_ salt

1 In a large bowl, beat together the eggs, egg yolks, garlic, and a good pinch of salt until well combined. (This can be done by hand or in a food processor.)

2 Add the oils very gradually at first, a little at a time, until the mixture thickens. At this stage, add the oils more generously until all the oil has become absorbed. (If the alioli splits or separates, put a tablespoon of cold water into a bowl and whisk in the split mixture a little at a time. Alternatively, beat an egg yolk in a bowl and again add the mixture little by little.)

3 Taste the alioli and add more salt, if it is necessary. A squeeze of lemon juice can also be added if you feel the taste needs to be sharpened.

Note_ This garlicky Catalan mayonnaise can be served as either a dip or sauce. Some suggestions follow.

Serving suggestions

PATATAS ALIOLI
Cook peeled new potatoes in plenty of salted water, drain, and toss with enough alioli to coat them. Sprinkle with a handful of chopped parsley and serve the potatoes warm.

DEEP-FRIED SQUID
Toss fresh squid rings in seasoned flour, then deep-fry in hot oil (375°F/190°C) for about 1 minute until golden and crispy. Serve each portion with ½ lemon, a sprinkling of coarse sea salt, and a dollop of alioli.

ZUCCHINI (COURGETTE) FRITTERS
Slice zucchini into batons. Prepare one bowl with 1½ cups (5oz/150g) seasoned all-purpose (plain) flour and another with 2 beaten eggs and 2 tablespoons of olive or vegetable oil whisked together. Coat the zucchini in the flour and then the egg mixture. Toss once more in the flour and deep-fry in hot oil (375°F/190°C) for 1 minute until golden. Serve with lemon wedges and plenty of alioli.

Pan amb tomat

Ingredients | *serves 4*

- 1 lb (500 g) plum tomatoes, ripe from the vine (if possible), cut into quarters
- 2 tsp superfine (caster) sugar
- olive oil for drizzling
- 4 slices crusty white bread
- 2–3 garlic cloves, peeled and halved
- handful basil leaves, freshly picked (if possible) and torn, to garnish
- salt

1 Preheat oven to 250°F (120°C/Gas Mark 1/2). Place the tomatoes, skin side down, on a baking sheet. Sprinkle with salt and sugar, then drizzle with olive oil.

2 Roast the tomatoes in the oven until they have become a deep red color and slightly shriveled, about 1 hour. Remove them from the oven.

3 To serve, place a portion of bread on each plate. Drizzle each one with olive oil, rub with garlic, and press the softened tomatoes on top. Garnish with torn basil.

Note _ If desired, the bread can be toasted first. Ciabatta is perfect or, alternatively, a sourdough.

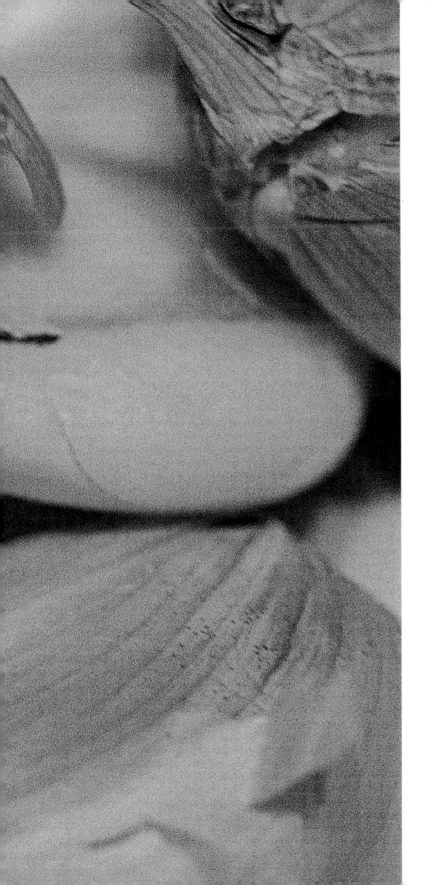

Vegetable dishes

42 Garlic baked plum tomatoes with lemon thyme, parsley & wilted arugula

45 Garlic and onion velouté

46 Roasted garlic empanaditas with blackened tomato chipotle sauce

50 Escalivada

53 Gratin of caramelized Belgian endives, smoked garlic & Comté cheese

54 Roasted garlic, tomatoes, olives, anchovies & crisp bread

Garlic-baked plum tomatoes with lemon thyme, parsley & wilted arugula

Ingredients | *serves 4*

- *16 medium plum tomatoes, ripe from the vine (if possible)*
- *2 tbsp clear honey (preferably Mexican)*
- *4 garlic cloves (preferably Elephant garlic), peeled and finely chopped*
- *5 tbsp extra virgin olive oil*
- *1 bunch lemon thyme, leaves picked*
- *1 tbsp balsamic vinegar (preferably 8-year-old)*
- *1 tsp soft brown (muscovado) sugar*
- *1 bunch flat-leaf parsley, leaves picked and chopped*
- *1 medium baguette, sliced into thick crostini*
- *4 good handfuls arugula (rocket), preferably wild*
- *1 cup (4oz/125g) shaved Parmesan cheese, to serve*
- *salt and freshly ground black pepper*

1 Preheat oven to 275°F (140°C/Gas Mark 1). Wash and core the tomatoes. Slice lengthwise in half and lay on a nonstick baking sheet, cut side up.

2 In a medium, heavy saucepan, gently warm the honey with the garlic and about 2 tablespoons of the olive oil until the mixture forms a liquid.

3 Brush the honey mixture generously over the halved tomatoes and sprinkle lemon thyme leaves over the top. Season with salt and pepper. Bake for 15 minutes to infuse and slightly cook the tomatoes without color. Set aside to cool.

4 Mix the balsamic vinegar and remaining olive oil together with the sugar and parsley in a stainless steel bowl to form a loose vinaigrette. Adjust the seasoning to taste.

5 Lightly toast the baguette slices on both sides and set aside to cool.

6 Wash and drain the arugula. Pat dry with paper towels. Place in a salad bowl and coat lightly with just enough dressing to taste.

7 To serve, divide the arugula among 4 plates. Place a portion of baked tomatoes on top of each pile of arugula and sprinkle with shaved Parmesan. Garnish with toasted baguette slices set to one side of the salad.

Garlic and onion velouté

1 To make the onion compote, select a large, heavy frying pan with a lid and melt the butter over low heat. Add the onions and water, together with a little salt. Cover and cook over medium heat until softened and without color, about 15 minutes. Add the garlic and cook until both ingredients become translucent and sweet (this is important because the velouté is a white, creamy soup), about 5 minutes. Season to taste and cover. Leave to cook for about 5 minutes.

2 At the same time as you are cooking the onions and garlic, heat the stock in a saucepan. Add the potatoes and cook slowly until the potatoes have softened, about 5 minutes.

3 Transfer the prepared compote to a large, deep, and heavy saucepan. Pour the stock and potatoes over the top and bring to a simmer. Add the heavy cream, then purée the soup in batches in a blender or food processor until smooth, 2–3 minutes altogether. Return to the pan and season to taste. Whisk lightly and leave to rest over low heat while you prepare the tortelloni.

4 Meanwhile, cook the pasta according to the directions on the package in boiling, salted water. Drain and keep warm while you pass the velouté through a large fine sieve and reheat it.

5 To serve, divide the pasta among 4 soup bowls and pour the velouté over the top. Drizzle with mustard oil and garnish with chervil sprigs. Serve immediately.

Ingredients | *serves 4*

- $1/2$ cup (4 oz/125 g) butter
- 8 oz (250 g) onions, finely sliced
- 2 tbsp water
- $2^{1}/_{2}$ oz (75 g) garlic cloves, peeled and finely sliced
- 2 cups (16 fl oz/500 ml) chicken stock
- 4 oz (125 g) new (waxy) potatoes such as Desiree or round red, peeled and finely sliced
- 1 cup (8 fl oz/250 ml) heavy (double) cream
- mushroom tortelloni (allow 4–5 oz/125–150 g per person or about 8 tortelloni each), to serve
- mustard oil (available from Asian stores), to serve
- 3–4 chervil sprigs, freshly picked if possible, to serve
- salt and freshly ground black pepper

vegetable dishes

Roasted garlic empanaditas with blackened tomato chipotle sauce

(recipe pictured overleaf)

Ingredients | serves 6–8

_ 4 cups (1¼ lb/625g) all-purpose (plain) flour, plus extra for rolling out
_ 1 tsp salt
_ ½ cup (4oz/125g) unsalted butter, cut into small pieces
_ ¾ cup (6 fl oz/180ml) cold water
_ egg wash (beat 1 egg and ¼ cup/2 fl oz/60ml milk together in a bowl)
_ 4 thyme sprigs, freshly picked if possible, to garnish
_ freshly ground black pepper

1 To make the pastry, sift the flour and salt together into a large mixing bowl. Add the butter and cut it into the flour using 2 forks until a coarse mixture resembling bread crumbs is achieved.

2 Add the water and work the mixture with your ands until a smooth dough is formed. Cover in plastic wrap and refrigerate for 30 minutes.

3 Meanwhile, to make the filling, preheat oven to 375°F (190°C/Gas Mark 5). Trim the top away from the garlic head to expose the tops of the cloves. Wrap in 2 layers of foil, place on a baking sheet, and then bake in the oven for 30 minutes. Remove and let cool. Keep the oven at the same temperature for baking the empanaditas.

4 While the garlic is baking, place the potatoes in a small, heavy saucepan and cover with cold, salted water. Bring to a boil, then reduce to a simmer and cook until tender when pierced with a fork, 30–45 minutes. Drain and transfer to a large mixing bowl.

5 Add the milk, butter, salt, and pepper to the potatoes. Separate the cloves from the roasted head of garlic. Squeeze each one into the potato mixture to free the sticky flesh.

6 Mash the potato mixture together until an even mixture is achieved (in this recipe, a few lumps are rather nice). Set aside.

7 To make the sauce, keep the oven at the same temperature. Place all the ingredients together in a bowl and toss to coat evenly with oil.

8 | Transfer to a baking sheet and place on the top rack of the oven until tomato skins start to blacken, about 15 minutes.

9 | Remove from the oven and place in a blender or food processor. Pulse for 15–20 seconds until a coarse purée is achieved. Set aside.

10 | To assemble the empanaditas, remove the pastry from the plastic wrap and knead on a clean, lightly floured surface for 20–30 seconds. Roll out to a thickness of about 1/2 in (3 mm).

11 | Use a cookie (biscuit) cutter, glass, or empty can to cut out as many 3 in (7.5 cm) circles as you can from the pastry. Brush egg wash onto one side of each circle.

12 | Place approximately 2 tablespoons of filling in the center of each circle, fold in half, and crimp the open edge with the tines of a fork in a decorative fashion.

13 | Pierce the top of each empanadita once with a fork, then brush with egg wash. Place on a baking sheet lined with parchment (greaseproof) paper and bake until golden brown, 12–15 minutes. Reheat the sauce gently while the empanaditas are baking.

14 | To serve, pour some of the hot sauce onto warmed plates and arrange the empanaditas on top (allow 3 per person). Garnish with fresh thyme sprigs and serve immediately.

for the filling

_ 1 garlic head
_ 2 medium potatoes (russet, if possible), peeled and quartered
_ 6 tbsp (3 fl oz/90 ml) skimmed milk
_ 1/4 cup (2 oz/60 g) butter, cut into pieces
_ salt and freshly ground black pepper

for the sauce

_ 10 plum tomatoes, ripe from the vine if possible, cored and halved
_ 1 large onion, chopped
_ 6 garlic cloves, peeled and finely chopped
_ 2 chipotle chiles (smoked jalapeños), seeded and finely chopped
_ 2 tbsp extra virgin olive oil
_ salt and freshly ground black pepper

Roasted garlic empanaditas
with blackened tomato chipotle sauce
(recipe on previous page)

Escalivada

Ingredients | serves 4-6

- 2 baking potatoes
- 2 small whole eggplants (aubergines), pricked all over with a fork
- 2 small onions (preferably yellow/Spanish), quartered (do not peel)
- 4 red bell peppers (capsicums), halved and seeded
- 6 tbsp (3 floz/90ml) olive oil, plus extra for drizzling
- 2 zucchini (courgettes), cut into batons
- crusty fresh bread slices, to serve
- salt and freshly ground black pepper

for the marinade

- 2/3 cup (1/4 pint/150ml) olive oil
- 4 garlic cloves, peeled and crushed
- 1 large bunch basil, leaves picked and torn

1 Preheat oven to 375°F (190°C/Gas Mark 5). Wrap the potatoes in foil and then bake until soft, about 1 hour.

2 Meanwhile, to make the marinade, in a large bowl, mix together the olive oil, garlic, basil, and a little sea salt. Set aside in a warm place until needed.

3 Once the potatoes are cooked, remove them from the oven. When cool enough to handle, peel and cut into bite-sized pieces; add to the marinade. Increase the oven temperature to 400°F (200°C/Gas Mark 6).

4 Place the remaining vegetables on a baking sheet. Sprinkle with salt and olive oil. Bake, uncovered, until soft, removing each vegetable when cooked. (The zucchini will take about 10 minutes; bell peppers and eggplants need about 30 minutes, and the onions should be done after 40–50 minutes.)

5 Add the zucchini batons to the marinade. Peel the baked bell peppers and onions and add to the marinade. Tear the eggplants into bite-sized pieces and add to the marinade.

6 To serve, toss the vegetables in the marinade until well coated. Season and serve at room temperature, accompanied by thick slices of crusty fresh bread to mop up all the juices.

Note _ Like Italian bruschetta, escalivada can be served on top of toasted bread, topped with olives and anchovies. It is also a good vegetable accompaniment to simply broiled (grilled) lamb chops (cutlets) or fresh cod.

Gratin of caramelized Belgian endives, smoked garlic & Comté cheese

1| If making your own garlic paste, preheat oven to 275°F (140°C/Gas Mark 1). Place the garlic bulb (with skin on) in a roasting pan for 20 minutes. When roasted, squeeze the flesh from the cloves into a bowl.

2| To prepare the Belgian endives, remove some of the white outer leaves and cut into thin strips. Place in acidulated water (water with lemon juice) for use as a garnish. Remove the remaining outer leaves and cut into quarters.

3| In a large, heavy frying pan over low heat, melt some butter and slowly brown the Belgian endive leaves over medium heat until golden brown, 3–4 minutes,. When colored, add the sugar and then enough vegetable stock to half cover the endive leaves. Continue cooking until the endive leaves are nicely glazed and the liquid has reduced. (The sugar helps to balance the bitter flavor.) Keep the leaves warm.

4| Slice the truffle, if using, and cut the chives into lengths of 2 in (5 cm).

5| Transfer the grated Comté cheese to a bowl. Add 1 tablespoon garlic paste or purée and mix together.

6| Place the caramelized endive leaves in a warmed heatproof serving dish. Sprinkle with the cheese and garlic mixture, then broil (grill) the surface until golden brown, 4–5 minutes, depending on the strength of the broiler (grill) and the dish.

7| To serve, divide the gratin among 4 plates. Sprinkle with chervil sprigs and chives, and top each with a truffle slice (if using). Serve immediately.

Note_ Ordinary garlic may be used in place of smoked in this recipe, but the flavor will not be as good.

Ingredients | serves 4

_ 1 tbsp smoked garlic paste or garlic purée (available in tubes)
_ 8 medium heads Belgian endive (chicory)
_ a little lemon juice
_ a little butter for frying
_ 1/4 cup (2oz/60g) sugar
_ about 1/2 cup (4 fl oz/125ml) vegetable stock (dilute 1/4 vegetable stock cube in boiling water according to the directions on the package)
_ 4 thin slices black truffle (optional)
_ 8 chive spears, to garnish
_ 1 cup (4oz/125g) grated Comté cheese
_ chervil sprigs, to garnish

Roasted garlic, tomatoes, olives, anchovies & crisp bread

Ingredients | *serves 4*

- 10 garlic cloves, peeled
- extra virgin olive oil, to taste
- 8 anchovy fillets
- 4–5 tbsp heavy (double) cream
- 4 sheets of carta di musica (Italian crisp bread), available from good delicatessens
- 4 large organic tomatoes or 12–16 cherry tomatoes
- 1/3 cup (2oz/60g) pitted black olives
- juice of 1/2 lemon
- salt and freshly ground black pepper

1| Preheat oven to 350°F (180°C/Gas Mark 4). Meanwhile, to make the bagna cauda (roasted garlic and anchovy sauce), finely chop 2 garlic cloves, place in a large, heavy saucepan, and add a good splash of olive oil. Cook over the lowest possible heat until the garlic melts, 20–30 minutes.

2| Add the anchovy fillets and continue to cook for a further 10 minutes until they form a paste with the garlic.

3| Now stir in the heavy cream, bring to a boil, and season. Set aside until needed.

4| Place the remaining garlic cloves in a shallow, heavy pan and cover with olive oil. Roast in the oven until golden brown, about 30 minutes.

5| Toast the carta di musica on both sides under a hot broiler (grill) until crisp and brown, about 1 minute.

6| Meanwhile, in a mortar with a pestle, smash the roasted garlic to a purée, then season with salt and pepper.

7| Spread the garlic purée onto the toasted carta di musica.

8| Cut the tomatoes in half and place them in a large bowl. Add the olives, some black pepper, a squeeze of lemon juice, and a splash of olive oil. Toss the mixture together.

9| To serve, transfer the carta di musica to individual serving plates, place some tomato mixture on top of each one, and drizzle with anchovy sauce. Serve immediately.

Note_ If you cannot obtain carta di musica, you can use any large, thin crisp breads instead.

Pasta & rice

58 | Goat cheese & chard cannelloni with garlic & rosemary sabayon

63 | Roasted sweet butternut squash risotto with new season's garlic & cilantro

64 | Orecchiette with vine-ripened cherry tomatoes & chorizo

67 | Wild garlic risotto

68 | Pennette with wild garlic, pine nuts, broccoli & Parmesan

70 | Chicken, chorizo & vegetable paella

73 | Penne with roasted garlic pesto

74 | Risotto with mussels, garlic, squid & shrimp

Goat cheese & chard cannelloni with garlic & rosemary sabayon

Ingredients | *serves 4 or 8*

- *1 cup (4oz/125g) good-quality pasta flour (preferably extra fine flour), plus extra for rolling out*
- *1 large egg*
- *1 tbsp olive oil, plus extra for cooking*
- *1 x 5-7oz (150-200g) fresh goat cheese log*
- *1 head Swiss chard, finely chopped*
- *1 smoked garlic bulb (available from good supermarkets or Italian delicatessens)*
- *4 red onions, finely sliced*
- *1 tomato, skinned (plunge into a bowl of boiling water first), seeded, and finely diced, to garnish*
- *4 tsp black olives, pitted, to garnish*
- *salt and freshly ground black pepper*

(recipe pictured overleaf)

1 To make the pasta dough, quickly mix together the flour, egg, olive oil, and salt in a large bowl (do not overwork). Cover in plastic wrap and let rest in the refrigerator for as long as possible, preferably overnight.

2 To make the garlic purée for the sabayon, preheat oven to 275°F (140°C/Gas Mark 1). Place the garlic bulb (skin on) in a roasting pan. Drizzle with olive oil and sprinkle with a little salt. Roast for 15 minutes and then squeeze out the flesh to make 1 tablespoon for this recipe.

3 For the filling, mix together the goat cheese and chard in another bowl. Season, then finely chop the smoked garlic; add to the bowl, and stir to combine. Divide the mixture into either 4 or 8 portions, depending on whether it is for an appetizer or main course.

4 On a floured work surface, roll the pasta out into one long sheet of about 2 x 1½ in (5 x 4 cm). Divide into 4 or 8 squares.

5 Bring a large, heavy saucepan of salted water to a boil and blanch the pasta, about 1 minute. Refresh in iced water. Spread a long sheet of plastic wrap out on the work surface. Put the pasta squares on top and let cool.

6 Place some filling in the center of each pasta square and roll up to form cannelloni shapes. As

the dough is quite sticky, the pasta tubes will seal together easily. Cover in plastic wrap and set aside in the refrigerator.

7 | To make the sabayon, in a large bowl, whisk together the egg yolks with the vinegar until stiff, 3–4 minutes. Stir in the cream and season to taste. Fold in the garlic purée and herbs.

8 | Warm some olive oil in a large, heavy frying pan and fry the onions until golden, 2–3 minutes.

9 | To serve, arrange the onions on serving plates. Heat the cannelloni through in the microwave for about 1 minute on full but keep checking as it cooks. Place on top of the onions. Spoon over some sabayon and quickly glaze under the broiler (grill), 1–2 minutes (again, keep checking). Garnish with diced tomato and olives, and serve immediately.

Note _ Serves 4 as a hearty main course or 8 as an appetizer. Smoked garlic gives this dish a really good flavor. If unavailable, ordinary garlic can be substituted. The pasta dough needs to be made up and left for as long as possible. To save time later on, you could make it the night before. If you don't have a microwave, bake the cannelloni, covered in foil, in an oven preheated to 350°F (180°C/Gas Mark 4) for 7–8 minutes.

for the sabayon

_ 1 tbsp garlic purée (use 1 garlic bulb, see step 2)
_ 6 egg yolks
_ 1 tbsp white wine vinegar
_ 7 tablespoons (3 1/2 fl oz /100 ml) semiwhipped heavy (double) cream
_ 1 tbsp finely chopped rosemary
_ 1 tbsp snipped chives

Goat cheese & chard cannelloni with
garlic & rosemary sabayon
(recipe on previous page)

Roasted sweet butternut squash risotto with new season's garlic & cilantro

Ingredients | serves 4

_ a little olive oil for frying
_ 500g/1lb butternut squash, peeled, seeded, and cut into ½ in (1 cm) dice
_ 4 cups (1¾ pints/1 liter) vegetable stock
_ 2 tbsp (1 fl oz/30ml) extra virgin olive oil
_ 1 large onion, finely sliced
_ 5 new season's garlic cloves (preferably Violetta), peeled and finely chopped
_ ¼ tsp ground cinnamon
_ 2 cups (14oz/400g) risotto rice (Arborio or Carnaroli, if possible)
_ ¼ cup (1oz/30g) freshly grated Parmesan cheese
_ ¼ bunch cilantro (coriander), leaves picked and chopped
_ salt and freshly ground black pepper

1 Heat a little olive oil in a large, heavy frying pan. Add the butternut squash and flash-fry until just softened and lightly colored. Remove and let cool on a rack.

2 In a large, heavy saucepan, bring the stock to a boil and then reduce the heat until barely simmering. Keep warm.

3 Place another saucepan over medium heat and warm the olive oil in it. Add the onion, chopped garlic, and cinnamon. Fry gently until the onion has softened without color, 3–5 minutes.

4 Add the rice to the saucepan and keep stirring until the rice is coated with olive oil and the edges are translucent. Add a ladleful of the hot stock and continue to stir over medium heat. As the rice absorbs the stock, add more stock but keep stirring to prevent the rice from sticking. Repeat until all the stock is added and the rice is tender but firm, about 20 minutes.

5 Add the panfried butternut squash, Parmesan, and cilantro to the risotto mixture. Adjust the seasoning to taste.

6 Divide the risotto among 4 plates and serve immediately.

Orecchiette with vine-ripened cherry tomatoes & chorizo

Ingredients | serves 4

- 5 tsp extra virgin olive oil, plus extra for drizzling
- 5 new season's garlic cloves, peeled and finely chopped
- 12 oz (375 g) chorizo, cut into ½ in (1 cm) dice
- 1 lb (500 g) cherry tomatoes, ripe from the vine (if possible), hulled and cut into halves
- 1 bunch basil, leaves freshly picked and coarsely chopped
- 1 cup (8 fl oz/250 ml) heavy (double) cream
- ¼ tsp celery salt
- 1 lb (500 g) package of orecchiette
- ¼ cup (1 oz/30 g) grated Parmesan cheese, to serve
- salt and freshly ground black pepper

1. In a large, heavy frying pan set over medium to low heat, warm the olive oil. Add the garlic and chorizo and fry slowly until the chorizo is lightly golden brown.

2. Add the cherry tomato halves and basil. Increase the heat to medium and cook, uncovered, until the tomatoes have softened, 5–6 minutes.

3. Reduce the heat, then stir in the cream and celery salt. Let the mixture simmer briefly until the liquid starts to thicken. Season with salt and pepper. Remove from the heat and set aside.

4. Meanwhile, fill a large, heavy saucepan with water. Add a little salt and some olive oil and bring to a boil. Add the pasta, then reduce the heat and cook until *al dente* (tender but firm to the bite), about 12 minutes or according to the package directions.

5. While the pasta is cooking, reheat the tomato-chorizo mixture gently over low heat.

6. Drain the pasta and return to the warm saucepan. Lightly drizzle with olive oil and season with salt and pepper. Add the sauce and toss until the sauce and pasta are combined.

7. To serve, divide among 4 serving bowls and serve immediately, sprinkled with grated Parmesan cheese.

Wild garlic risotto

1| In a large, heavy saucepan, heat the olive oil. Add the onion and sweat until translucent, about 5 minutes.

2| With a wooden spoon, stir in the rice and a ladleful of hot vegetable stock. When all the liquid has been absorbed, add another ladleful of stock and cook until it, too, has been absorbed. Continue to add the stock in this way until the rice is almost cooked, 15–18 minutes.

3| Rinse and coarsely chop the garlic leaves and toss them into the pan. Season, stir, and continue to cook for a further 2 minutes. By this time the rice should be nice and creamy but still *al dente* (firm to the bite) in the middle.

4| Remove the pan from the heat and beat in the butter and Parmesan cheese.

5| To serve, divide the risotto among 4 plates and serve immediately.

Note _ This is a rustic dish that is best enjoyed without any additional flavorings or accompaniments. Wild garlic gives it a distinctive taste. If unavailable, do not substitute ordinary garlic.

Ingredients | serves 4

_ 1/4 cup (2 fl oz/60 ml) olive oil
_ 1 medium onion, finely chopped
_ 1 cup (7 oz/200 g) risotto rice (Arborio or Carnaroli if possible)
_ 4 cups (1 3/4 pints/1 liter) hot vegetable stock
_ 3 oz (90 g) wild garlic leaves
_ 1/2 cup (4 oz/125 g) unsalted butter
_ 1/4 cup (2 oz/60 g) grated Parmesan cheese
_ salt and freshly ground black pepper

Pennette with wild garlic, pine nuts, broccoli & Parmesan

Ingredients | *serves 4*

- 1 lb (500g) pennette (small penne)
- 2 tbsp olive oil
- 8 oz (250g) broccoli, cut into small florets
- 4 oz (125g) arugula (rocket), leaves picked
- 4 oz (125g) baby spinach, leaves picked
- grated Parmesan cheese, to serve
- salt and freshly ground black pepper

for the pesto sauce

- 6 tbsp pine nuts
- ½ bunch basil, leaves picked
- 4 oz (125g) garlic cloves (preferably wild), peeled
- 2 tbsp grated Parmesan cheese
- ⅔ cup (¼ pint/150ml) olive oil

1 To make the pesto, toast the pine nuts in a dry frying pan over low heat, turning frequently, until golden, 2–3 minutes. Place 2 tablespoons in the bowl of a food processor (reserve the rest for the garnish), together with the basil leaves, garlic cloves, Parmesan cheese, and olive oil. Blend until smooth, 2–3 minutes.

2 To cook the pasta, fill a large, heavy saucepan with water. Bring to a boil and then add 1 tablespoon salt. Add the pasta, reduce the heat, and let simmer for about 10 minutes (or according to the directions on the package) until *al dente* (firm to the bite). Drain (reserve a ladleful of the cooking water) and keep warm.

3 Heat the olive oil in a large, heavy frying pan and sauté the broccoli, about 2 minutes. Add the cooked pasta and toss together for about 30 seconds.

4 Stir in the prepared pesto and reserved cooking water; cook for 1 further minute. Toss in the arugula and baby spinach. Stir the mixture through, season, and divide among 4 plates. Garnish with the reserved pine nuts and serve immediately with a bowl of grated Parmesan.

Note _ The pesto may be made in advance and stored in a sealed jar in the refrigerator for 2–3 weeks.

Chicken, chorizo & vegetable paella

Ingredients | *serves 4*

- 4 tbsp olive oil
- 1 medium chicken, cut into 4 serving pieces
- 1 large onion (preferably yellow/Spanish), chopped
- 4 tomatoes, skinned (plunge into boiling water) and diced
- 4 garlic cloves, peeled, finely chopped, and crushed
- 3¾ cups (1½ pints/900ml) chicken stock, or dissolve 2 chicken stock cubes in water
- 5oz (150g) chorizo, thinly sliced
- ½ tsp saffron
- ½ tsp paprika
- 1 cup (7oz/200g) paella or risotto rice
- 4oz (125g) haricot verts (fine French beans), tips removed
- 4oz (125g) shelled fava (broad) beans
- 4oz (125g) spinach, shredded

1 To make the paella, heat the olive oil in a large paella pan or shallow flameproof casserole over medium heat.

2 Brown the chicken pieces in the pan, about 10 minutes. Add the onion, tomatoes, and garlic to the pan. Sweat together for about 20 minutes.

3 Add the stock to the pan and bring to a boil. At the boiling point, add the remaining ingredients, stir gently, and then reduce the heat and let simmer for about 15 minutes. (At this stage the rice should be soft but retain a little bite. You should not need to stir the mixture at all, but if you do, stir gently.)

4 Remove the pan from the heat, cover, and let stand for about 5 minutes before serving.

5 To serve, divide among 4 serving plates and serve immediately.

Penne with roasted garlic pesto

1| Preheat oven to 350°F (180°C/Gas Mark 4). Meanwhile, rinse the potato (keep the skin on) and bring to a boil in a large, heavy saucepan of salted water. Reduce the heat and let simmer until three-quarters cooked, about 10 minutes. Drain and let cool in a colander.

2| Place the garlic bulbs, unpeeled, in a shallow roasting pan and drizzle the olive oil liberally over them. Bake in the oven for 40 minutes. Remove and let cool in the pan.

3| Coarsely chop the herbs and potato, then transfer to a mortar. Press out each clove of the cooling garlic into a bowl to produce a sticky purée. Transfer to the mortar. Gradually add olive oil (use some of the infused oil left over from roasting) and seasoning. Grind with a pestle until the pesto reaches a rough, spreading consistency.

4| Bring a large, heavy saucepan of salted water to a boil and cook the penne until *al dente* (firm to the bite), 8–10 minutes depending on quality

5| Drain the cooked pasta and place in a large bowl. Add the pesto and toss the ingredients together to coat the pasta. Season to taste.

6| Divide among 4 plates and serve immediately. This simple peasant dish is already rich and full of flavor from the roasted garlic and herbs and is best served plain.

Ingredients | *serves 4*

_ 1 small baking potato
_ 4 garlic bulbs
_ scant 1 cup (7 fl oz / 200 ml) olive oil
_ 2 bunches basil, freshly picked (if possible)
_ 1 bunch flat-leaf parsley, freshly picked (if possible)
_ 14oz (400g) good-quality penne
_ salt and freshly ground black pepper

Note_ To add gloss to the pasta, drizzle some of the infused oil into the saucepan. Toss the pasta in the oil before adding the pesto.

Risotto with mussels, garlic, squid & shrimp

Ingredients | serves 4–6

- 1lb (500g) mussels, beards removed and scrubbed
- 4 cups (1¾ pints/1 liter) water or fish stock, make up to the full amount with the strained mussel juice, see Steps 1 and 2
- 6 tbsp (3oz/90g) unsalted butter
- 3 tbsp olive oil
- 1 onion, finely chopped
- 5 garlic cloves, peeled and finely chopped
- 2 cups (14oz/400g) risotto rice (Arborio or Carnaroli, if possible)
- 1 cup (8floz/250ml) dry white wine
- 8oz (250g) squid, ink sacs removed, cleaned, peeled, blanched, and cut into small pieces (ask your fishmonger to do this for you or blanch for 1 minute in acidulated water)
- 8oz (250g) peeled shrimp (prawns)
- 5 plum tomatoes, skins removed, seeded, and chopped
- 3 tbsp finely chopped parsley
- a crisp salad, to serve
- salt and freshly ground black pepper

1 | First cook the mussels. Heat a large, heavy saucepan with a tight-fitting lid until hot. Add the mussels and cover with the lid. Shake the pan well. Leave to cook for 4–5 minutes over high heat to allow the mussels to open up, then shake the pan again. Remove the lid to check that all the mussels have opened. If not, cook for a further 4–5 minutes with the lid on until the shells have opened. Discard any mussels that still remain closed at this stage.

2 | Drain the mussels, but add the juices to the stock. If you prefer to serve mussels without shells, allow them to cool a little before removing the meat; set aside. Strain the cooking juices through a sieve to remove any leftover sand or shell pieces and transfer to the stock or water. Keep warm.

3 | In a large, heavy saucepan, heat two-thirds of the butter with the olive oil. When it starts to foam, fry the onion and garlic together for 3–4 minutes. Add the rice and warm through before pouring in the wine.

4 | Allow the wine to evaporate a little, then add the stock, a ladle at a time, stirring continuously between each addition (ensure that the liquid has been almost entirely absorbed before adding the next ladleful). Halfway through the cooking process, stir in the squid, and just before the last ladle of stock, stir in the mussels, shrimp, chopped tomatoes, parsley, and the remaining butter. Check the seasoning and adjust to taste (this depends on the saltiness of the mussels).

5 | To serve, spoon into pasta bowls and serve immediately with a crisp side salad.

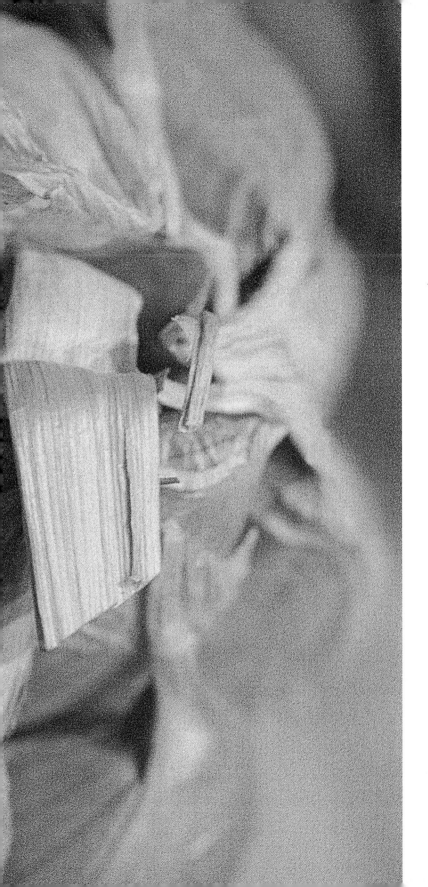

Fish & seafood

78 | Seared salt-cured salmon with porcini crust & celeriac & garlic purée

80 | Monkfish with turmeric, dill & onion

82 | Sardines filled with pesto potatoes & tomato salsa

86 | Salmon ceviche

89 | Pan-seared scallops with garlic purée & deep-fried parsley

90 | Crispy squid with bitter lemon

93 | Shrimp wontons with spicy sweet & sour sauce & Hawaiian salsa

94 | Spiced raw tuna with Moroccan tabbouleh

96 | Smoked haddock with aioli potatoes & garlic chips

100 | Steamed skate with wild garlic & oyster mushrooms

102 | Shrimp chermoula

106 | Monkfish studded with young garlic, saffron tagliatelle & fennel sauce

108 | Black mussels with Thai red curry broth

112 | Tagine of lobster with couscous & garlic confit

114 | Brandade of cod with garlic bruschetta

Ingredients | serves 4

- ½ bunch thyme, leaves picked and chopped
- 3 garlic cloves, peeled and chopped
- 2 tbsp sea salt
- 4 salmon fillets, skinned
- a little vegetable oil and butter for frying
- handful of arugula (rocket) leaves, to garnish
- 1 lemon, cut into wedges
- 1 tbsp aged balsamic vinegar (10-year-old, if possible)

for the celeriac & garlic purée
- 2 garlic bulbs
- 1 head celeriac
- 3 baking potatoes
- scant 1 cup (7floz/200ml) heavy (double) cream
- ½ cup (4oz/125g) butter

for the porcini crust
- 2oz (60g) dried porcini mushrooms
- ½ bunch dried thyme
- 1¼ cups (5oz/150g) bread crumbs
- 1 tsp freshly ground black pepper
- 1 egg white, beaten

Seared salt-cured salmon with porcini crust & celeriac & garlic purée

1 To marinate the salmon, in a bowl mix together the fresh thyme, garlic cloves, and salt. Coat the salmon fillets with the mixture, cover in plastic wrap, and refrigerate for 24 hours.

2 Rinse the coating from the fillets and let soak in a bowl of cold water for 1 hour, changing the water twice.

3 Preheat oven to 375°F (190°C/Gas Mark 5). To prepare the purée, wrap the garlic bulbs in some foil, then bake in the oven until soft, about 15 minutes. Remove, separate, and peel when cool enough to handle. (Keep the oven at the same heat while you finish off the purée and prepare the salmon.)

4 Meanwhile, peel the celeriac and potatoes. Bring to a boil separately in salted water and let simmer for about 20 minutes or until tender. Transfer the roast garlic, cooked potatoes, and celeriac to the bowl of a food processor and process to form a purée.

5 Place the cream and butter in a large, heavy saucepan and slowly bring to a boil over low heat, stirring occasionally. Remove from the heat and whisk into the purée. Set aside but keep warm.

6 To prepare the salmon, in a food processor or bowl, mix together the porcini, dried thyme, bread crumbs, and pepper. Brush one side of each salmon fillet with egg white and coat with the crust mixture.

7 Warm a large, heavy frying pan, then melt a little vegetable oil and butter. Fry the salmon, crust side down, until golden, 2–3 minutes. Turn and bake in the oven for 2–3 minutes (this dish should be served quite rare).

8 To serve, place a spoonful of purée in the center of each plate and top with a salmon fillet. Arrange a few arugula leaves and a lemon wedge on the side. Drizzle with balsamic vinegar and serve immediately.

Note_The salmon needs to be marinated 24 hours in advance of the main recipe.

Monkfish with turmeric, dill & onion

1 | Cut the monkfish into ½ in (1 cm) slices.

2 | To make the marinade, in a blender or food processor, finely grind the galangal (or ginger). Transfer to a large bowl and add the yogurt, garlic, and turmeric. Mix together thoroughly.

3 | Stir in the sliced monkfish pieces and leave to marinate, covered in the refrigerator, for 4 hours.

4 | Heat some vegetable oil in a hot frying pan and fry the monkfish until golden, 3–4 minutes.

5 | Add the onion slices and dill, and stir for 1 minute.

6 | To serve, divide among 4 plates and serve immediately with lime halves.

Ingredients | *serves 4*

- *4 lb (2 kg) monkfish tail, filleted and skinned (ask your fishmonger to do this for you)*
- *1 small stem (about 1 oz/30 g) galangal (if unavailable, replace with peeled ginger but use half the amount)*
- *scant 1 cup (7oz/200g) Greek plain yogurt*
- *2 garlic cloves, peeled and minced to a purée*
- *3 tbsp turmeric powder*
- *sunflower oil for frying*
- *2 large onions, finely sliced*
- *8 dill sprigs, chopped into thirds (including the stem)*
- *2 limes, halved, to serve*

Sardines filled with pesto potatoes & tomato salsa

(recipe pictured overleaf)

1 Preheat oven to 400°F (200°C/Gas Mark 6). Meanwhile, in a blender or food processor, place all the ingredients for the pesto filling apart from the potatoes. Blend to form a purée, about 3 minutes, season, and set aside until needed.

2 To make the filling for the sardines, place the potatoes in a large, heavy saucepan. Cover with water and add a little salt. Bring to a boil, then let simmer for 10 minutes until very soft, but not overcooked (until a knife can be pushed through them).

3 Transfer the potatoes to a large mixing bowl, mash with a fork, and then stir in the pesto. Season, if required.

4 Fill each of the filleted sardines with the pesto-potato mixture, then season with salt and pepper. Line a baking sheet with parchment (greaseproof) paper, place the sardines on top, and drizzle with olive oil. Roast, uncovered, in the center of the oven, 5–6 minutes. To keep the surface of the fish shiny and glazed, baste frequently with the cooking juices. When cooked, the sardines should be slightly firm and lightly brown.

5 Meanwhile, to make the salsa, transfer the diced tomatoes to a large mixing bowl. Add the diced shallot and garlic. Mix together, then season with salt, pepper, and lemon juice. Finally, stir in the olive oil.

6 To serve, divide the salsa among 4 plates. Place the roasted sardines on top and garnish with herb sprigs. Serve immediately.

Note_The pesto can be made in advance and stored in a screw-topped jar in the refrigerator. It will keep for 3 weeks.

Ingredients | *serves 4*

- 12 sardines, descaled and filleted (remove the head, guts, and bones but leave the tail joining the two halves; ask your fishmonger to do this for you)
- a little olive oil for drizzling
- 1 small bunch herbs (basil, parsley, and chives), leaves picked, to garnish
- salt and freshly ground black pepper

for the pesto potatoes
- 1 bunch basil, freshly picked (if possible)
- 1 garlic clove, peeled
- 1/4 cup (1oz/30g) grated Parmesan cheese
- 1/4 cup (1oz/30g) pine nuts
- 1/4 cup (2floz/60ml) extra virgin olive oil
- 7oz (200g) boiling potatoes, peeled and quartered
- salt and freshly ground black pepper

for the salsa
- 4 plum tomatoes, skins removed (plunge into boiling water first), seeded, and finely diced
- 1 shallot, finely chopped
- 1 garlic clove, peeled and finely chopped
- juice of 1 lemon
- 5 tsp extra virgin olive oil (fruity and not too strong)

Sardines filled with pesto potatoes & tomato salsa
(Recipe on previous page)

Salmon ceviche

Ingredients | *serves 4*

- *1 large sweet potato, washed and scrubbed*
- *olive oil for drizzling*
- *12 oz (375 g) skinless salmon fillet, diced to 1/2 in (1 cm)*
- *1 small bunch cilantro (coriander), leaves picked, to garnish*
- *salt and freshly ground black pepper*

for the dressing

- *1 thumb-sized piece of smooth ginger, peeled*
- *3 garlic cloves, peeled*
- *2/3 cup (1/4 pint/150 ml) lemon juice (about 4 large, juicy lemons)*
- *4 tbsp extra virgin olive oil*
- *1 large red chile (chilli), seeded and finely chopped*
- *4 scallions (spring onions), trimmed and finely sliced at an angle into 1 1/2 in (4 cm) pieces*

1 Preheat oven to 400°F (200°C / Gas Mark 6). Slice the sweet potato into 4 thick pieces, discarding the narrow ends. Place in a large, heavy saucepan of salted water and bring to a boil. Reduce the heat and let simmer until soft but not mushy, 10–15 minutes. (Use a knife to test for doneness like a regular potato.)

2 Drain the sweet potato and place in a roasting pan with some olive oil and seasoning. Roast until golden brown, turning once, 5–10 minutes. Let stand in the roasting pan. (This will keep the sweet potato just above room temperature, perfect for serving.)

3 Meanwhile, to make the dressing, use the finest part of the grater to grate the ginger and garlic into a bowl. Add the lemon juice, olive oil, chile, and scallions. Season with salt and pepper.

4 Place the fish in a deep-sided tray and pour enough dressing over the top so the fish moves around freely but is not drowned in dressing. Let rest at room temperature, about 20 minutes.

5 To serve, divide the roasted sweet potato among 4 plates and spoon the fish mixture on top. Sprinkle with cilantro leaves and serve immediately.

Note_ This dish is served as an appetizer. You can add lots of different vegetables to make it into a main meal. Try sugar snap peas, avocados, green beans, and/or salad greens.

Pan-seared scallops with garlic purée & deep-fried parsley

1 Place the garlic cloves and potatoes in a large, heavy saucepan. Stir in the lemon juice, season, and cover with water. Bring to a boil, then reduce the heat to simmering point. Cook until the potatoes and garlic have completely softened, about 20 minutes. Drain and return to the saucepan. Blend lightly with the cream and keep warm.

2 Pick the parsley. Wash and pat dry with paper towels. Heat the oil in a deep-fat fryer to 265°F (130°C) and deep-fry the parsley until crisp but still green, 30 seconds to 1 minute. Remove the parsley from the oil and drain on paper towels.

3 Meanwhile, quickly season the scallops. Heat the olive oil in a large, heavy frying pan and sear the scallops, about 1 minute on each side.

4 To serve, pile the creamy potato mixture on each plate. Place a portion of scallops on top and garnish with the deep-fried parsley. Serve immediately.

Ingredients | serves 4

- 6 garlic cloves, peeled
- 3 new potatoes, peeled and cut in half
- juice of 1 lemon
- 7 tbsp (3 1/2 fl oz / 100 ml) heavy (double) cream
- 10 flat-leaf parsley sprigs, freshly picked (if possible)
- vegetable oil for frying
- 20 small scallops, prepared and cleaned (ask your fishmonger to do this for you)
- 1/4 cup (2 fl oz / 60 ml) olive oil
- salt and freshly ground black pepper

Crispy squid with bitter lemon

Ingredients | serves 4

- 3 garlic cloves
- 1 bunch dill, freshly picked (if possible)
- 6 tbsp fish sauce
- 1lb (500g) cleaned squid rings and tentacles (4 medium squid tubes)
- 1 tbsp ground black peppercorns
- 4 tbsp all-purpose (plain) flour
- 4 tbsp cornstarch (cornflour)
- a little vegetable or sunflower oil for deep frying
- 1 cup (8floz/250ml) dressing (see below)

for the garnish
- 4 limes, cut into quarters or halved

for the dressing
- 2 limes
- 3 lemons
- 1 bunch mint, freshly picked (if possible)
- 1 cup (8floz/250ml) bottled bitter lemon juice
- ¼ cup (2oz/60g) superfine (caster) sugar

1| To make the dressing, use a sharp knife to carefully remove the rind from the limes and lemons. Juice the fruit and discard the seeds.

2| Wash the mint and set aside to drain. In a large, heavy saucepan, warm the juice of the fresh fruit and the bitter lemon juice together. Do not allow the mixture to boil.

3| Stir in the superfine sugar, remove from the heat, and continue stirring until the sugar has dissolved. Let cool. To serve, finely shred the mint leaves and add to the cooled dressing.

4| To prepare the squid, peel the garlic cloves and rinse the dill. Roughly chop the two together in a blender or food processor. Transfer to a large bowl and stir in the fish sauce.

5| Stir in the squid and peppercorns. Cover and leave to marinate for at least 6 hours in the refrigerator.

6| In a large bowl, mix together the flour and cornstarch. Remove the squid from the marinade with a slotted spoon and coat it thoroughly in the flour mixture.

7| Heat some oil in a deep-fat fryer and fry the squid until crispy, about 3 minutes. Drain on paper towels.

8| To serve, arrange the squid on 4 individual plates on tempura paper, if available. Garnish with lime quarters or halves and serve with small dipping bowls of the dressing.

Note _The dressing needs to be made at least 1 day in advance to allow the mint to infuse. It may be stored, covered, in the refrigerator for up to 2 weeks. The squid and peppercorns should be left to marinate for at least 6 hours in the refrigerator. This recipe can also be served as a side dish.

for the sweet & sour sauce

- ½ cup (4oz/125g) sugar
- 1 tbsp red wine vinegar
- ¼ cup (2floz/50ml) rice wine vinegar
- 1 tbsp white wine vinegar
- 2 tsp low-sodium soy sauce
- ½ tsp red chile (chilli) flakes
- ½ tsp ground cinnamon
- ½ tsp finely chopped garlic

for the marinade

- ½ cup (4floz/125ml) low-sodium soy sauce
- ½ cup (4floz/125ml) sesame oil
- ½ cup (1oz/30g) loosely packed cilantro (coriander), freshly picked (if possible)
- 1 lemongrass stalk, trimmed and finely chopped
- 1 thumb-sized piece ginger (about 2oz/60g), peeled
- ½ medium egg
- ½ garlic clove, peeled

Shrimp wontons with spicy sweet & sour sauce & Hawaiian salsa

1 To make the salsa, place all the ingredients in a large bowl and mix together. Cover with plastic wrap and chill for 2 hours.

2 For the marinade, place all the ingredients in a blender or food processor. Process together, about 2 minutes.

3 Place the shrimp in a large, shallow bowl and pour over the marinade. Cover and set aside for 15 minutes.

4 Meanwhile, place all the ingredients for the sweet & sour sauce in a large, heavy saucepan over low heat. Cover and let simmer for 20 minutes, stirring occasionally. Keep warm.

5 To assemble the wontons, lay the wrappers out flat on a worktop, and place a basil leaf at one end of each wrapper. Top each basil leaf with a shrimp and roll up to form cigar shapes. Brush with a little egg white to seal.

6 Heat the vegetable oil in a deep-fat fryer to 350°F (180°C) and deep-fry the wontons until they become crisp and the shrimp inside each one is lightly cooked, 1 1/2 – 2 minutes. Drain on paper towels.

7 To serve, arrange the wontons on plates, ladle some sauce over the top, and place a spoonful of salsa on the side of each one. Garnish with hoisin sauce and chives, and serve immediately.

Note _ The salsa can be made a day in advance and can be stored, covered, in the refrigerator for a day.

Ingredients | serves 4

- 12 large shrimp (prawns), peeled and cleaned, heads and tails removed
- 12 wonton wrappers (available from Asian stores)
- 12 basil leaves
- egg white for sealing
- vegetable oil for deep-frying
- 1/2 cup (4floz/125ml) hoisin sauce (squirt directly from the bottle), to garnish
- snipped chives, to garnish

for the salsa

- 1 large, ripe mango, peeled, pitted, and finely diced
- 1/2 medium onion, finely diced
- 1/4 cup (1/2 oz/15g) loosely packed cilantro (coriander), freshly picked (if possible) and chopped

Spiced raw tuna with Moroccan tabbouleh

Ingredients | serves 4

- 1 tsp paprika
- 3 tsp ground cumin
- 3 tsp ground coriander
- 1 tsp Ras-El-Hanout (available from North African spice stores or by mail order)
- 1 tsp harissa
- 1 tsp garlic purée (blend 5 peeled garlic cloves in a little olive oil to combine)
- 1 lb (500 g) bluefin tuna loin, cut into thick steaks, pinboned, and skin removed (ask your fishmonger to do this for you or slice the skinned loin yourself)
- ½ lime, to serve
- shichimi spice (Japanese spice blend available from Japanese stores or by mail order), to serve
- lemon olive oil for drizzling

for the tabbouleh

- 1 bunch flat-leaf parsley, leaves picked
- ½ bunch mint, leaves picked
- ½ red onion, cut into ¼ in (5 mm) dice
- 2 scallion (spring onion) bulbs, cut into ¼ in (5 mm) dice
- 2 plum tomatoes, seeded and cut into ¼ in (5 mm) dice
- 3 tbsp bulgur wheat
- juice of 1 lemon
- 4 tsp extra virgin olive oil
- sea salt

1 | To make the tabbouleh, finely chop the parsley and mint. Mix together in a large bowl. Stir in the onion, scallion, tomatoes, and bulgur wheat, then pour in the lemon juice and olive oil. Season with salt to taste, then stir all the ingredients together.

2 | Cover the bowl with plastic wrap and refrigerate until ready to serve.

3 | For the tuna, mix all spices together in a shallow bowl. Brush the surface of the tuna with the garlic purée, then roll to coat the fish in the spices.

4 | Preheat the broiler (grill) to very hot and broil (grill) the tuna on both sides until the spices are browned, about 30 seconds on each side. (The tuna meat should still be raw in the middle.)

5 | To serve, thinly slice the tuna and arrange 5 pieces in a fan shape around each plate. Place a good heaped tablespoonful of tabbouleh in the middle of each fan. Cut the lime into wedges and place by the side of the tabbouleh. Sprinkle a good pinch of shichimi spice around the edge of each plate, drizzle with lemon olive oil, and serve immediately.

Smoked haddock with aioli potatoes & garlic chips

Ingredients | serves 4

- 1 x 1lb (500g) smoked haddock fillet, pinboned, trimmed, and cut into 4 pieces (ask your fishmonger to do this for you)
- milk for poaching (enough to cover the fish)
- ½ bay leaf
- 2 thyme sprigs, freshly picked (if possible)
- 1 tbsp olive oil for frying
- 1 shallot, finely chopped
- 2 tsp sherry vinegar
- 4 new potatoes, boiled, then peeled and sliced
- 2 tbsp aioli (see below)
- 2 tbsp finely chopped chives
- salt and freshly ground black pepper

for the garlic chips
- canola (rapeseed) oil for deep-frying
- 4 garlic cloves, peeled and finely sliced

This recipe makes 4 generous appetizer portions and will also serve 4 as a light main course. Poach the haddock about an hour ahead of the remaining recipe.

1 To make the aioli, blanch 4 garlic cloves (skin on) in boiling water until soft, 4–5 minutes for new season's garlic, longer for older garlic. Squeeze the flesh out of the skins into the bowl of a food processor.

2 Peel the remaining garlic clove and add this to the bowl. (The raw garlic adds strength to the aioli.) Add the mustard and raw and hard-boiled egg yolks. Purée until smooth, about 30 seconds.

3 Add both the oils slowly through the funnel of the food processor and process to form an emulsion, 2–3 minutes.

4 Season and stir in the lemon juice and Pernod. Cover and refrigerate until needed.

5 To poach the haddock, place it in a large, heavy saucepan. Pour over enough milk to cover the fish. Add the bay leaf and thyme. Bring to a boil over gentle heat, then remove from the heat and cover with a plate. Set aside until tepid, about 1 hour.

6 Heat the olive oil in a large nonstick frying pan. Remove the fish from the saucepan and sear lightly on both sides, 30 seconds to 1 minute. Set aside and keep warm.

7 To make the aioli potatoes, add the shallots to the pan and fry until soft. Deglaze with sherry vinegar. Add the cooked new potatoes and crush the mixture with a fork. Season and keep warm.

8 For the salad, pick the leaves and place in a bowl together with the cress. Toss in vinaigrette and set aside.

9 To make the garlic chips, heat some canola oil in a deep-fat fryer and fry the garlic cloves at 265°F (130°C) until golden crisp, about 1 minute. Drain on paper towels.

10 Sprinkle the snipped chives into the aioli and stir together. Add to the pan with the potatoes and shallot. Stir gently to bind all the ingredients together.

11 To serve, place a portion of the potato/aioli mixture in the center of each plate in a circle. Place the seared haddock on top and arrange the dressed salad on top. Sprinkle garlic chips around each plate and serve immediately.

Note_If you want to make the aioli in advance, it can be stored, covered, in a glass container or ramekin in the refrigerator. Aioli made with raw eggs will keep refrigerated for up to 2 days, but aioli made from pasteurized eggs will last for up to a week in the refrigerator. Any remaining aioli can be served with cold meats.

for the salad
- 1 bunch arugula (rocket), preferably wild
- 1 head frisée
- 2 small bags or baskets (punnets) mustard cress or other peppery cress
- 4 tsp freshly made vinaigrette

for the aioli
(makes $2/3$ cup/ $1/4$ pint/150ml)
- 5 garlic cloves
- 1 tsp Dijon mustard
- 1 raw egg yolk
- yolk of 1 hard-boiled egg
- $1/2$ cup (4 fl oz/125 ml) extra virgin olive oil
- $1/2$ cup (4 fl oz/125 ml) canola (rapeseed) oil
- juice of $1/4$ lemon
- $1/2$ tsp Pernod
- salt and freshly ground black pepper

steamed skate with wild garlic & oyster mushrooms
(recipe on following page)

Steamed skate with wild garlic & oyster mushrooms

(recipe picture on previous page)

Ingredients | *serves 4*

- *1 x 1lb (500g) skate wing, skinned and deboned (ask your fishmonger to do this for you)*
- *handful of sliced green garlic leaves*
- *finely chopped cilantro (coriander) and garlic flowers, to garnish*
- *salt and freshly ground black pepper*

1| To prepare the fish, lay the skate out flat on a work surface, then season and place a layer of garlic leaves on top. Roll up lengthwise and secure with toothpicks (cocktail sticks). Set aside.

2| For the sauce, heat a large, heavy frying pan, then add the olive oil. Fry the garlic with the chile and thyme until softened and without color. Pour in the chicken stock and let simmer for about 20 minutes.

3| Remove the thyme and chile from the sauce. Pass through a fine sieve into a large bowl, then stir in the panko flakes to thicken the mixture. Season to taste and set aside.

4| To prepare the mushrooms, melt the butter in a large, heavy frying pan. Add the chile, lemongrass, and shallot. Fry in the butter until softened, about 1 minute.

5| Add the mushrooms to the pan and sauté until tender, about 3 minutes. Season to taste and keep warm.

6| In a bamboo steamer (available from Asian stores), cook the skate roll until just opaque throughout, about 5 minutes. Meanwhile, gently reheat the sauce.

7| To serve, place a portion of mushrooms in the center of each plate and garnish with cilantro. Pour the sauce around the mushrooms. Divide the skate into 4 portions and arrange vertically with the mushrooms. Garnish with garlic flowers and serve.

for the sauce
- 3 tbsp olive oil
- 1 garlic clove, peeled and finely sliced
- 1 Thai red chile (chilli), seeded and finely diced
- 1 thyme sprig
- 1 1/3 cups (10floz/300ml) chicken stock
- 2–3 tbsp panko flakes (Japanese bread crumbs), available from Asian stores

for the mushrooms
- 1 tbsp butter
- 1 Thai red chile (chilli), seeded and finely chopped
- 1 lemongrass stalk, trimmed and finely chopped
- 1 shallot, finely chopped
- 500g (1 lb) oyster mushrooms

Ingredients | serves 4

- ¼ cup (2 fl oz/60 ml) olive oil
- 20 tiger shrimp (prawns), butterflied (see below)
- 8 oz/250 g cherry tomatoes, ripe from the vine, halved
- 10 oz (300 g) baby eggplants (aubergines), halved and deep-fried in olive oil (4–5 minutes until the edges are crisp)
- 1 quantity chermoula butter (see below)
- 8 oz (250 g) arugula (rocket)
- scant 1 cup (7 fl oz/200 ml) lemon olive oil
- salt and freshly ground black pepper

for the chermoula butter

- ½ bunch cilantro (coriander), leaves picked
- 3 garlic cloves, peeled
- 2 large red chiles (chillies), seeded
- juice of 1 lemon
- 1 cup (8 oz/250 g) butter, softened

Shrimp chermoula

1 | To make the chermoula butter, place the cilantro leaves, garlic, and chiles, together with the lemon juice, in a blender or food processor and process together, 1–2 minutes. Add the butter, season, and process again, 2–4 minutes. Set aside until needed.

2 | Heat a large, heavy frying pan, then add the olive oil. Sear the shrimp until almost cooked (they will become pink), 3–4 minutes. Add the cherry tomatoes and baby eggplant halves. Then add the chermoula butter and stir-fry until softened, about 2 minutes. Keep warm.

3 | To serve, build up a salad tower on each plate. Divide the arugula among the plates, add 5 shrimp per plate, some cherry tomatoes, and eggplants. Drizzle with lemon olive oil and serve.

Note_To butterfly shrimp, devein them first, then peel halfway to leave a little shell remaining on the tail. Finally, cut the peeled part in half lengthwise. Alternatively, ask your fishmonger to do this for you.

Monkfish studded with young garlic, saffron tagliatelle & fennel sauce

(recipe on following page)

Monkfish studded with young garlic, saffron tagliatelle & fennel sauce

Ingredients | serves 4

- 8 garlic cloves, peeled
- 1 large monkfish tail, cleaned and filleted (ask your fishmonger to do this for you)
- 1 tbsp butter
- 1 tbsp olive oil
- salt and freshly ground black pepper

for the saffron oil

- 2 cups (16 fl oz/500ml) extra virgin olive oil
- 4 pinches of saffron

for the tagliatelle

- 3 cups (1 lb/500g) sifted all-purpose (plain) flour, plus extra for rolling out
- 1 tsp salt
- 5 eggs
- 1 tbsp olive oil

(recipe picture on previous page)

1 To prepare the oil, in a large, heavy saucepan, warm the olive oil with the saffron. Leave to infuse for several hours before use.

2 For the pasta, put the flour and salt in the bowl of a food processor. Add the eggs and oil, and pulse until the pasta starts to come together as a loose ball of dough. Knead on a lightly floured surface until smooth, about 3 minutes.

3 Divide the pasta into 8 pieces and briefly knead the individual balls. Cover in plastic wrap and refrigerate for at least 20 minutes, and up to 2 hours.

4 To prepare the dough for cutting into tagliatelle, put it through a pasta machine, following the manufacturer's instructions. Alternatively, hand-knead and hand-roll the equivalent of passing it through the machine 10 times. (Do this in a cool place so that the pasta does not dry.)

5 For the sauce, melt the butter in a large, heavy frying pan over medium to high heat. Sweat the monkfish bones in the butter until they begin to fall apart. Add the onion and fennel and fry until soft but without color, 3–5 minutes.

6 Stir in the wine and cream, and let simmer for 5 minutes. Remove the bones from the sauce and blend in a food processor or blender until smooth. Season and set aside.

7| Preheat oven to 350°F (180°C/Gas Mark 4). Slice the garlic into slivers and use a very sharp knife to cut small slits in the monkfish. Stud the monkfish with the garlic. Place in a roasting pan and season with salt and pepper. Dot with butter and drizzle with olive oil, then roast until the fish is lightly colored, about 10 minutes.

8| Meanwhile, bring a large, heavy saucepan of salted water to a boil and cook the tagliatelle until *al dente* (firm to the bite), 3–5 minutes. Reheat the sauce in the pan and thicken with a little more butter and olive oil. Drain the pasta, toss in the prepared saffron oil, and season.

9| To serve, pour some sauce onto each plate. Add a nest of noodles and top with 2 slices of monkfish. Sprinkle with coarse sea salt and serve immediately.

Note_ Allow plenty of time to infuse the saffron oil and prepare the tagliatelle.

for the sauce

_ 1 tbsp butter, plus extra to thicken
_ 10oz (300g) monkfish bones
_ 1 onion, finely diced
_ 1 large head of fennel, trimmed and diced
_ 1 cup (8 fl oz/250ml) white wine
_ 2/3 cup (1/4 pint/150ml) heavy (double) cream
_ a little olive oil, to thicken

Black mussels with Thai red curry broth

Ingredients | *serves 4*

- 1 tbsp peanut (groundnut) oil
- 1 tsp minced ginger
- ½ tsp minced garlic
- ½ tsp Thai red curry paste
- 1 tbsp lemongrass, finely chopped
- 1 tsp minced shallot
- 1½ lb (750g) black mussels, beards removed and scrubbed
- ¼ cup (2 fl oz / 60 ml) sake
- ½ cup (4 fl oz / 125 ml) coconut milk
- 1 tsp butter
- salt, to serve

1 | Heat a large, heavy frying pan over medium heat. Pour in the peanut oil and when hot, add the ginger, garlic, curry paste, lemongrass, and shallot. Sauté for 10 seconds, shaking the pan occasionally.

2 | Add the mussels (still in their shells), sake, coconut milk, and butter, cover, and cook until the shells open, about 3 minutes. Discard any unopened mussels, then season to taste.

3 | To serve, turn the mussels in their sauce out into 4 soup bowls and serve immediately.

Tagine of lobster with couscous & garlic confit
(recipe on following page)

110_ **fish & seafood**

Tagine of lobster with couscous & garlic confit

Ingredients | serves 4

- 2 garlic bulbs
- 2/3 cup (1/4 pint/150ml) duck fat
- about 5 cups (2 pints/1.2 liters) vegetable stock, enough to cover the lobster
- 4 medium, live lobsters
- a little butter
- 4 carrots, peeled
- 1/2 head celeriac, peeled
- 2 zucchini (courgettes)
- olive oil for frying
- 2/3 cup (4oz/125g) couscous
- a pinch of saffron
- 1/2 tbsp small baby onions, peeled and blanched (plunge into boiling water for 2–3 minutes)
- 1/2 tbsp cooked chickpeas
- 1/2 tbsp golden raisins (sultanas) (place in a pan of cold water and bring to a boil, then refresh to plump up)
- 6–7 spinach leaves
- salt and freshly ground black pepper

(recipe picture on previous page)

1 Preheat oven to 275°F (140°C/Gas Mark 1). Place the garlic bulbs (skin on) in a roasting pan with the duck fat. Slow-roast for 20 minutes while you prepare the other ingredients.

2 To cook the lobsters, in a large, heavy saucepan, heat the vegetable stock. When hot, add the lobsters. Take the pan away from the heat and leave the lobsters to cook in the stock for 4–5 minutes (be careful not to overcook). Remove from the pan and plunge into iced water to arrest the cooking process. When cold, use a heavy, sharp knife to remove the tails from the shells and carefully remove the claws to keep them in one piece. Cut the tails in half. Trim the heads with sharp scissors (around the line near the head); reserve for decoration.

3 Place the prepared lobsters in a large, heatproof dish with a little butter and set aside.

4 For the sauce, in a small, heavy saucepan, infuse the chicken stock with the harissa over low heat, 10–15 minutes. Pass through a small sieve to remove any lumps. Leave, covered, in the pan.

5 Slice the carrots, celeriac, and zucchini into disks about 1/2 in (1 cm) wide and 1/4 in (5 mm) thick. Heat some olive oil in a large, heavy frying pan and fry the couscous until coated in oil. Quickly moisten with 1/4 cup (2 fl oz/60 ml) boiling water and remove the pan from the heat. Season with saffron, salt, and pepper. Cover the pan with plastic wrap and leave to steam for 5 minutes.

6 In a large, heavy saucepan, heat a little oil or butter and fry the carrots, celeriac, and zucchini, together with the baby onions, chickpeas, and golden raisins until just cooked, 4–5 minutes. Heat a small pan and rinse the spinach leaves. Quickly wilt in a little butter and water (this takes a few seconds); drain.

7 Place an equal portion of spinach in 4 individual (2 in/5 cm in diameter) metal ring molds. Add a layer of couscous, packing it in quite tightly, and top with the fried vegetable mixture.

8 Warm a tagine (or other heatproof platter) in the oven and turn the filled molds out onto it. Decorate with the reserved lobster heads and keep warm.

9 To serve, quickly warm the lobster tails and claws under a preheated broiler (grill), 2–3 minutes, and warm through the sauce over low heat, 2–3 minutes. Brush the tails and claws with olive oil and place on the tagine dish. Finally, add the roasted garlic cloves (these can be eaten directly from their skins). Pour the warmed sauce around the tagine and serve.

Note_ For best results, use live lobsters in this recipe, as they will be fresher.

for the sauce
_ ¼ cup (2 fl oz/60 ml) reduced good-quality chicken stock
_ ¼ tsp harissa (Moroccan hot sauce)

Brandade of cod with garlic bruschetta

Ingredients | *serves 4*

- 12oz (375g) cod fillet, skin on
- 4 cups (1¾ pints/1 liter) milk
- ½ garlic bulb
- 1 thyme sprig, freshly picked (if possible)
- 8oz (250g) boiling potatoes
- ½ cup (4fl oz/125ml) extra virgin olive oil (fruity, but not too strong), plus extra to garnish
- ⅓ cup (3fl oz/90ml) heavy (double) cream
- 4 slices olive bread
- salt and freshly ground black pepper

for the salad

- 1 bunch mixed salad leaves of your choice, such as arugula (rocket) and cilantro (coriander)
- balsamic vinaigrette, to serve

1 To make the brandade, place the cod in a large, heavy saucepan. Pour the milk over the top and add the unpeeled garlic and thyme. Sprinkle with a little sea salt to taste. Over low heat, poach the fish in the milk, 4–7 minutes depending on size. Carefully remove the cod from the milk and transfer to a large plate. Peel the garlic (the skin can now be removed quite easily) and crush slightly to release the juices.

2 Remove the skin and bones from the cod, then break it up into flakes with a fork. Meanwhile, boil the potatoes in their skins in salted water until soft, 20–30 minutes. Strain and leave to dry out in their own steam for a few minutes, then peel.

3 Transfer the flaked cod to the bowl of a food processor. Add the potato flesh to the bowl. (Alternatively, transfer the cod and potato flesh to a large mixing bowl and combine with the ingredients in step 4 with your hands.)

4 In a small, heavy saucepan, heat the olive oil. Add the hot oil to the bowl of the food processor, together with the cream. Season with salt and pepper, then add crushed garlic to taste (reserve 1 clove for the bruschetta). Blend together for 1–2 minutes until combined, but do not purée.

5 Under a preheated broiler (grill), toast the olive bread lightly on both sides, about 1 minute. Rub with the remaining clove of garlic.

6 To serve, spread each slice of toasted bread with brandade and divide among 4 plates. Garnish with a little olive oil and serve immediately with a salad of mixed leaves dressed in a balsamic vinaigrette.

Note_Toasted olive bread rubbed with garlic is known as crostini in Italy. It can be used as a base for all kinds of toppings, including prosciutto.

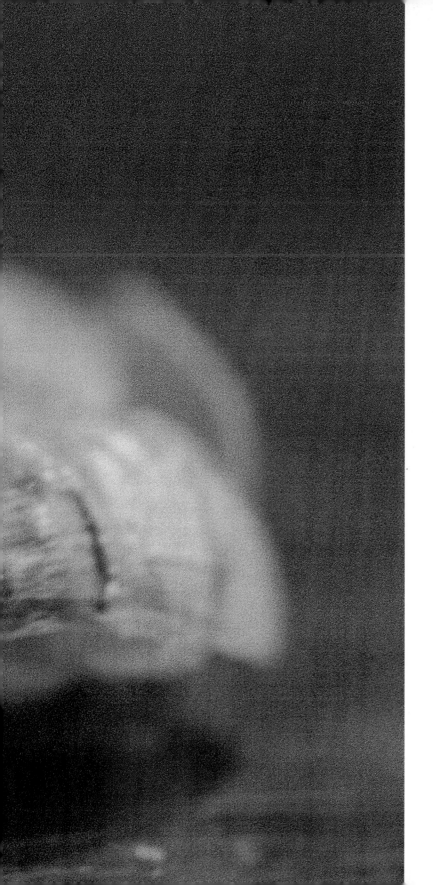

Poultry & meats

119 | Sesame lamb & shiitake sauté with mint & shallots

120 | Grilled pita bread filled with lamb, garlic & thyme

122 | Chicken baked in sea salt with garlic

126 | Squab with sweet garlic

128 | Roast lamb with roast garlic & rosemary potatoes

132 | Broiled rib-eye steak with tomato, eggplant & chickpeas garnished with zaatar

136 | Roast leg of lamb with Provençal vegetables & skordalia

139 | Roast chicken with fresh borlotti beans and aioli

140 | Blackened garlic & goat cheese stuffed quail

142 | Garlic & red chile-rubbed rack of lamb with ancho & sun-dried cherry compote

145 | Broiled Catalonia chorizo salad with Manchego cheese, garlic chips, arugula & black olives

147 | Pan-seared foie gras on Asian pear salad with shiso & roasted garlic brioche

148 | Spicy garlic chicken laksa

150 | Chicken Kiev style with baby leeks & mashed potato

Sesame lamb & shiitake sauté with mint & shallots

1| Shred the meat into thin strips. The smaller the pieces, the easier the lamb will be to marinate and cook.

2| Peel and chop the garlic and ginger.

3| In a large shallow dish, combine the garlic, ginger, 6 tablespoons of the soy sauce, and the sesame oil. Leave the lamb to marinate in it, covered, for about 6 hours in the refrigerator.

4| Peel the shallots and then finely slice them lengthwise.

5| Chop the bok choy into small pieces; wash it and leave to drain. Wipe and finely slice the mushrooms.

6| In a large, heavy frying pan, dry-roast the sesame seeds (there is sufficient oil inside them already) until golden, about 2 minutes. Grind the seeds and let cool.

7| Pick the leaves from the mint and wash and dry them.

8| Heat a dry wok and, when hot, remove the lamb from the marinade and add to the wok (the oil from the marinade is sufficient for frying). Fry until sealed all over, about 2 minutes. Add the mushrooms, shallots, and bok choy.

9| When the mixture is almost cooked, after about 3 minutes, add the remaining soy sauce and stir. Just before serving stir in the mint leaves. Arrange the sauté on a serving dish and sprinkle with ground sesame seeds.

Ingredients | serves 4

_ 14 oz (400 g) lamb cut from leg or loin, trimmed of fat and sinews removed (ask your butcher to do this for you)
_ 2 garlic cloves
_ 1 thumb-sized piece ginger
_ 1 cup (7 fl oz / 200 ml) light soy sauce
_ 4 tsp sesame oil
_ 3 large shallots
_ 4 heads bok choy (pak choy)
_ 4 oz (125 g) shiitake or oyster mushrooms
_ 2 tbsp sesame seeds
_ 1 bunch mint, freshly picked (if possible)

Grilled pita bread filled with lamb, garlic & thyme

Ingredients | *serves 4*

- 12oz (375g) ground (minced) lamb with at least 15% fat
- 1 heaped tbsp thyme, freshly picked (if possible) and finely chopped
- 1 garlic clove, peeled and crushed to a paste
- 8 pita breads
- pure olive oil for brushing
- salt and freshly ground black pepper

for the salad
- 4 plum tomatoes
- ½ cucumber
- 6 scallions (spring onions), trimmed
- 10 mint leaves, freshly picked (if possible) and finely chopped
- 3 tbsp extra virgin olive oil
- juice of 1 lemon

1 To prepare the filling, in a large bowl, mix the lamb together with the thyme and garlic. Season with salt and pepper.

2 With a sharp knife, split the pita breads, butterfly style, to make pockets to hold the filling. (Leave one side to act as a hinge.)

3 Spread a layer of the meat mixture, about ½ in (1 cm) thick, over the inside of one pita half, close the pita, and repeat as necessary to fill each of the pitas. Lightly brush each one with olive oil, cover with plastic wrap, and refrigerate until needed (up to 24 hours). (If the bread is left unwrapped, it will go stale very quickly.)

4 To make the salad, dice the tomatoes, cucumber, and scallions, about ½ in (1 cm) thick. Transfer to a large mixing bowl, add the mint, and toss the ingredients together. Season with olive oil and lemon juice to taste. Set aside until needed.

5 Preheat the broiler (grill) until hot. Meanwhile, remove the filled pitas from the refrigerator. Broil (grill) for at least 2 minutes on each side until crisp and brown. (Alternatively, barbecue for a few minutes each side.)

6 To serve, cut each pita into 4 finger pieces. Place on individual serving plates and add a side serving of salad.

Ingredients | serves 4

- 1 organic free-range chicken
- 40 garlic cloves, peeled
- 2 rosemary sprigs, freshly picked (if possible)
- about 2 lb (1 kg) coarse sea salt (enough to cover the chicken)
- 1 2/3 cups (14 fl oz / 400 ml) chicken stock
- salt and freshly ground black pepper

for the roasted beets
- 24 small beets (beetroot), cleaned and scrubbed to remove any grit, with a little stem remaining
- 3–4 garlic cloves, peeled
- a few thyme sprigs, freshly picked (if possible)
- extra virgin olive oil, to taste

for the salsa verde
- 1 tbsp capers
- 1/3 garlic clove, peeled
- 1 small bunch each: flat-leaf parsley, mint, and basil, freshly picked (if possible)
- 1 tsp Dijon mustard
- extra virgin olive oil and white wine vinegar, to taste

Chicken baked in sea salt with garlic

(recipe pictured overleaf)

1| To make the horseradish sauce, place the grated horseradish in a mixing bowl.

2| Pour the olive oil into a shallow bowl. Add a little stale bread and leave to soak. Squeeze the oil out of the bread and repeat until you have enough bread to equal the size of an egg.

3| Chop the egg and bread together and place in the bowl with the horseradish. Stir in a good splash of olive oil to form a sauce, then add a good splash of white wine vinegar and season. Set aside, covered in the refrigerator, until needed.

4| To make the salsa verde, in a food processor (or by hand), finely chop the capers, garlic, and herbs together.

5| Add the mustard, a splash of olive oil, and white wine vinegar and season to taste. Mix together to form a thick green paste.

6| To bake the chicken, preheat oven to 350°F (180°C / Gas Mark 4). Stuff the chicken with the garlic cloves and rosemary. Take a heavy, lidded Dutch oven (casserole), which is large enough to hold the chicken, and cover the base with about 1 in (2.5 cm) salt. Add the chicken and completely cover it with salt. Splash some water over the top of the chicken to moisten the first layer and cover the pot with foil.

7| Place the lid on top of the pot. Warm the pot base over low heat on top of the stove for a few minutes, then bake the chicken in the oven for 1 hour.

8| While the chicken is baking, place the beets in a large roasting pan with the garlic cloves, thyme, a good splash of olive oil, and a little water. Cover with foil and bake for about 20 minutes.

9| Remove the pot from the oven and let stand for 15–30 minutes. Remove the lid, crack the salt away from the surface, and lift the chicken out onto a rack. Wipe away any excess salt and remove the skin.

10| When the beets are ready, you should be able to prick each one with a knife, but they should still be firm. Remove the foil and return the pan to the oven to allow them to dry out a little. Meanwhile, warm through the stock.

11| To serve, divide the chicken among 4 plates and pour over a little stock. Serve immediately with the roasted beets, salsa verde, and horseradish sauce.

Note _ The horseradish sauce can be prepared in advance and stored in a sealed jar in the refrigerator for 4–5 days. It is difficult to make salsa verde in small quantities. Store any salsa left over from this recipe in a sealed jar and keep refrigerated for up to 7 days. It is a nice accompaniment to broiled (grilled) meat or fish.

for the horseradish sauce
_ 1 stick horseradish, peeled and grated to make 2–3 tbsp
_ scant 1 cup (7 fl oz / 200 ml) extra virgin olive oil, plus extra to taste
_ 1 small slice stale bread, torn into pieces
_ 1 hard-boiled egg, peeled
_ white wine vinegar, to taste

Chicken baked in sea salt with garlic
(recipe on previous page)

Squab with sweet garlic

Ingredients | serves 4

- 4 x 15 oz (450 g) squab (pigeons), trimmed, cleaned, and trussed (ask your butcher to do this for you)
- 2 garlic cloves
- 1/2 cup (4 oz/125 g) butter, plus 1/2 tbsp butter for frying
- 1 shallot, peeled
- 1 small bunch thyme, freshly picked (if possible)
- 1/4 cup (2 fl oz/60 ml) Armagnac
- 3 tbsp red wine
- 3 tbsp chicken stock
- roasted garlic cloves, to serve
- salt and freshly ground black pepper

1| Preheat oven to 450°F (230°C/Gas Mark 8). Meanwhile, to prepare the squab, season the inside and outside of each bird. Blanch the garlic cloves, unpeeled, in a large, heavy saucepan of boiling water. Repeat this procedure 7 times in fresh batches of boiling water to reduce the strength of the garlic and make it smooth tasting.

2| Place the squab, uncovered, preferably in a cocotte or a small, heavy roasting pan and dot with butter. Sprinkle with blanched garlic. Roast gently until the skin is slightly golden, about 14 minutes. Glaze the birds frequently with buttery pan juices using a tablespoon.

3| Remove the birds from the oven and check the seasoning. Let rest for 10 minutes and keep the garlic cloves warm.

4| Debone the squab (slice the breasts cleanly away, then remove the bones from the legs, taking out the larger bone first) and reserve the meat; set the bones to one side.

5| Meanwhile, use a sharp knife to mince the shallot into small cubes. Wash the thyme and break the squab bones into small pieces.

6| To make the sauce, in a large, heavy saucepan, melt 1/2 tablespoon butter. Add the minced shallot and the squab carcasses. Deglaze the pan and flame with Armagnac, followed by the red wine. Reduce the liquid to one-half, add the chicken stock, reduce again, then add the thyme; reduce again by half.

7| Strain the sauce through a very fine sieve into a large, heavy saucepan. Press the bones firmly to obtain all the juices and taste of the squab; keep hot. Warm through the squab breasts once more and glaze the meat with the cooking juices.

8| To serve, place 2 squab breasts on each plate and decorate with the garlic cloves. Serve the hot sauce in a separate sauceboat.

Roast lamb with roast garlic & rosemary potatoes

(recipe pictured overleaf)

Ingredients | serves 6

- 2 lb (1 kg) boneless lamb sirloin (chump)
- 7 tbsp (3½ fl oz / 100 ml) olive oil
- ½ bunch mint, freshly picked (if possible), finely chopped
- ½ bunch flat-leaf parsley, freshly picked (if possible), finely chopped
- juice of 1 lemon
- salt and freshly ground black pepper

1 | To prepare the gravy, pour the stock into a large, heavy saucepan and stir in the red wine. Let thicken over low heat and then add the lamb bones and just enough water to cover them.

2 | Stir in the reserved rosemary stalks, peppercorns, and roasted garlic. Let simmer for 2–3 hours over very low heat.

3 | Pass the stock through a large sieve into another pan and reduce over medium heat until dark and shiny. Set aside.

4 | To roast the lamb, preheat oven to 375°F (190°C/Gas Mark 5). With a sharp knife, score the fatty surface in a crisscross pattern and season with plenty of salt. Place a large roasting pan over low heat and pour in the olive oil. When hot, add the lamb, skin side down, and quickly fry to seal the surface all over until golden brown, about 5 minutes. Sprinkle with herbs and lemon juice. Season and transfer to the oven. Roast, uncovered, for about 40 minutes (turn halfway through).

5 | While the lamb is roasting, peel the potatoes and cut into quarters. In a large, deep roasting pan, heat the goose fat, dripping, or vegetable oil. Cook about three-quarters of the garlic cloves over medium heat until very soft, about

5 minutes. Remove with a slotted spoon and discard. Add half the rosemary leaves to the pan and cook gently for 2–3 minutes. Remove with a slotted spoon and discard.

6 | Add the potatoes to the pan, season, and sprinkle with the remaining rosemary and garlic. Roast, uncovered, for about 20 minutes until golden and tender, turning occasionally. Remove from the oven and keep warm.

7 | Remove the lamb from the oven, let rest for 5 minutes, then slice. Meanwhile, gently reheat the gravy. (Add a few tablespoons of cooking juices from the meat and potatoes for extra flavor.)

8 | To serve, divide the lamb among 6 plates. Add the potatoes and drizzle with gravy. Serve immediately.

Note _ The stock can be prepared the day before, but if time is limited, substitute a ready-made one. Similarly, the preparation for the gravy can be done the day before and stored, covered, in the refrigerator.

for the gravy

_ 7 tbsp (3 1/2 fl oz / 100 ml) lamb, chicken or vegetable stock
_ 1 glass red wine
_ lamb bones (reserved from lamb sirloin)
_ stalks from 1 bunch rosemary (see below)
_ 1 tsp crushed black peppercorns
_ 3–4 roasted garlic cloves, peeled

for the garlic & rosemary potatoes

_ 8 large potatoes
_ 1 lb (500 g) goose fat or beef drippings, (or 7 tbsp/3 1/2 fl oz / 100 ml vegetable oil)
_ 3 garlic bulbs, cloves separated and peeled
_ 1 bunch rosemary, leaves picked (reserve the stalks)

poultry & meats _ 129

Roast lamb with roast garlic & rosemary potatoes
(recipe on previous page)

Broiled rib-eye steak with tomato, eggplant & chickpeas garnished with zaatar

Ingredients | serves 4

- vegetable oil for frying
- 2 lb (900 g) eggplants (aubergines), sliced lengthwise (skin on) into 2 x 1/2 in (5 x 1 cm) batons
- 1 lb (500 g) cherry tomatoes, ripe from the vine (if possible)
- 5 garlic cloves, peeled and crushed
- 2 small (14 oz/400 g) cans chickpeas, rinsed and drained
- 1/4 bunch cilantro (coriander), leaves picked
- 4 x 8 oz (250 g) rib-eye steaks, trimmed
- 1 lemon
- salt and freshly ground black pepper

for the zaatar

- 1/2 bunch thyme
- 1/2 bunch oregano, leaves picked
- 2/3 cup (2 oz/60 g) sesame seeds
- 4 tsp sumac (available from Middle Eastern or North African stores and by mail order from specialty spice outlets)
- sea salt

1 To dry the herbs for the zaatar, place in a pan in the center of a very low oven, 140°F (60°C) for 2–3 hours. Remove from the oven and let cool.

2 Meanwhile, in a dry, heavy frying pan over high heat, toast the sesame seeds until golden, 1–2 minutes. Let cool.

3 Transfer the herbs and sesame seeds to a blender or food processor. Add the sumac and sea salt to taste, then blend until a fine powder forms, 2–3 minutes. Set aside.

4 In a large deep-fat fryer, heat some vegetable oil, to 265°F (130°C) and deep-fry the eggplants until a dark brown crispy edge forms (they should still be soft in the middle), 4–5 minutes.

5 Cut the tomatoes in half, then add to the fryer with the garlic and fry until crisp on the outside, 2–3 minutes. Drain on paper towels and add to the eggplants.

6 Add the chickpeas to the eggplant and tomato mixture. Then stir in the cilantro leaves, reserving a few for the garnish.

7 Season each steak with a good pinch of zaatar and broil (grill) to taste, (about 4 minutes for rare; 6–7 minutes for medium; and 8–9 minutes for well done on each side). Slice and let rest for 3–4 minutes.

8 To serve, pile the chickpea mixture onto each plate. Garnish with some of the cilantro leaves and top each one with a steak. Sprinkle lightly with extra zaatar and top with a few more cilantro leaves. Slice the lemon into wedges, add a wedge to each plate, then serve immediately.

Roast leg of lamb with Provençal vegetables & skordalia

(recipe on following page)

Roast leg of lamb with Provençal vegetables & skordalia

(recipe picture on previous page)

Ingredients | *serves 8*

_ 1 x 6lb (3kg) leg of lamb
_ 2oz (60g) garlic, peeled and sliced into fine slivers
_ ¼ cup (2floz/60ml) extra virgin olive oil
_ salt and freshly ground black pepper

The rich flavors of the Provençal vegetables match the sweet flavors of spring lamb, while the earthy skordalia provides a creamy medium for the flavors to mingle. The vegetables may also be served with beef, veal, and robust fish such as tuna and red mullet.

1 To roast the garlic for the skordalia, preheat oven to 350°F (180°C/Gas Mark 4). Wrap the garlic in foil, place in a roasting pan, and roast for 2 hours. Let cool, then squeeze the golden brown pulp from the center into a bowl; discard the husks.

2 Blend the garlic with the juice of 1 lemon and ¼ cup (2 fl oz / 60 ml) of the extra virgin olive oil until smooth to form a purée. Set aside while you roast the lamb and prepare the vegetables.

3 Preheat oven to 475°F (240°C/Gas Mark 9). (The temperature needs to be this high to allow the lamb to caramelize and become nice and moist, but still pink in the middle.) Make small slits all over the surface of the lamb with a sharp knife and insert the garlic slivers.

4 Rub the lamb with salt and olive oil, and then roast it, uncovered, for 45 minutes. Remove the lamb from the oven, wrap it in foil, and then let it rest in a warm place for 20 minutes. This will relax the meat and continue the cooking process so that the meat is cooked all the way through.

5 To prepare the vegetables, cut the eggplants into slices about ½ in (1 cm) thick and discard the centers. Dice into squares of about ½ in (1 cm), then rinse, sprinkle with the salt, and set aside to drain for 30 minutes.

6 Plunge the tomatoes into a bowl of boiling water, then skin, seed, and finely dice.

7 | Seed and finely dice the red bell peppers. Then peel and dice the onions and finely mince the garlic. Pick the basil and parsley leaves.

8 | Rinse and finely chop the anchovies. Rinse and pat the diced eggplant dry with paper towels.

9 | Heat the oil in a deep-fat fryer to 375°F (190°C). Fry the basil and parsley leaves until crisp, about 30 seconds. Transfer to a large bowl, then reheat the oil. When hot, fry the eggplant until golden, about 5 minutes; transfer to the bowl.

10 | Pour a little of the oil into a frying pan and place over medium heat. Fry the onions and garlic together until transparent, about 3 minutes. Add to the bowl. Then fry the bell peppers until soft, about 5 minutes, and transfer to the bowl. Finally, fry the anchovies, capers, and olives. Let simmer for 1 minute, then remove from the heat, and add to the vegetable mixture. Adjust the seasoning and toss the vegetables together. Set aside.

11 | To make the skordalia, peel and boil the potatoes. Mash and combine with the prepared garlic and the juice of 2 lemons. Slowly stream the remaining oil into the bowl, whipping the mixture with a wooden spoon until it reaches the consistency of mayonnaise; season and keep warm.

12 | To serve, warm the vegetables through and divide among 8 plates. Carve the lamb into slices and place a portion on top of each pile of vegetables. Top with the skordalia and serve.

Note _ Skordalia is a Greek garlic sauce that varies from region to region. It often contains ground almonds and raw garlic. This version is made with roast garlic for a more subtle flavor, and it is cleaner and smoother without the almonds. The garlic purée is a versatile recipe that can be used in salad dressings or sauces or served as an accompaniment to goat cheese.

for the vegetables

- 7 oz (200 g) eggplants (aubergines)
- ¼ cup (2 oz / 60 g) sea salt
- 7 oz (200 g) plum tomatoes, ripe from the vine (if possible)
- 7 oz (200 g) red bell peppers (capsicums)
- 5 oz (150 g) onions
- 1 oz (30 g) garlic cloves, peeled
- 1 bunch basil, freshly picked (if possible)
- 2 oz (60 g) flat-leaf parsley
- 2 oz (60 g) anchovy fillets in salt or olive oil
- 1 cup (8 fl oz / 250 ml) extra virgin olive oil
- 2 oz (60 g) baby capers
- 4 oz (125 g) Arbequina or other good-quality black olives

for the skordalia

- 7 oz (200 g) garlic bulbs
- 3 lemons
- 1 cup (8 fl oz / 250 ml) extra virgin olive oil
- 1 lb (500 g) russet or other baking potatoes

Roast chicken with fresh borlotti beans & aioli

1 Preheat oven to 400°F (200°C/Gas Mark 6). Rub the chicken breasts with butter and season with salt and pepper. Place the chicken in a roasting pan and roast, uncovered, in the oven for 25 minutes. Remove and let rest in a warm place while you prepare the salad and aioli.

2 To make the salad, place the beans in a large, heavy saucepan of cold water. Bring slowly to a boil, reduce the heat, and let simmer gently until the beans are cooked but firm, about 20 minutes.

3 Drain and refresh the beans in cold water immediately. Then drain again.

4 Plunge the tomatoes into a bowl of boiling water, then peel, seed and finely chop. Set aside.

5 Peel and finely chop the shallots. Heat some oil in a large, heavy frying pan, then add the shallots and a pinch of salt. Fry the shallots slowly until translucent, about 5 minutes. Remove from the heat and let cool.

6 In a large bowl, combine the beans, shallots, olive oil, tomatoes, garlic, parsley, baby chard leaves, and lemon juice. Adjust the seasoning with salt and pepper. Set aside until needed.

7 To make the aioli, pound the garlic and a pinch of salt in a mortar with a pestle.

8 Transfer to a large mixing bowl and combine with the egg yolk and lemon juice.

9 Whisk in the olive oil until the aioli has the same consistency as thick mayonnaise. Cover and refrigerate until needed.

10 To serve, place a pile of salad on each plate. Slice the meat from the chicken breasts and place on the salad. Spoon some aioli on top and season with pepper. Serve immediately.

Note_ Any shelling beans, such as borlotti or cranberry beans, can be used in this light summer dish. Aioli, a classic garlic sauce that epitomizes all the flavors of Provence, lends a creamy texture and adds a sharp, acidic flavor to the salad. The salad can also be served as an accompaniment to any other poultry or broiled (grilled) fish. If you wish to make the aioli in advance, it can be stored, covered, in the refrigerator for 1–2 days.

Ingredients | serves 4

_ 4 chicken breasts, preferably corn-fed
_ 2/3 cup (5oz/150g) butter, softened at room temperature
_ salt and freshly ground black pepper

for the bean salad

_ 2/3 cup (4oz/125g) shelled fresh borlotti beans
_ 5oz (150g) plum tomatoes, ripe from the vine (if possible)
_ 4oz (125g) shallots
_ 7 tbsp (3 1/2 floz/100ml) extra virgin olive oil, plus extra for frying
_ 2oz (60g) garlic, peeled and finely chopped
_ 2oz (60g) flat-leaf parsley, freshly picked (if possible), chopped fine
_ 5oz (150g) baby chard leaves
_ juice of 1 lemon

for the aioli

_ 2oz (60g) garlic cloves, peeled
_ 1 large egg, separated
_ juice of 1 lemon
_ 1 cup (8 floz/250ml) extra virgin olive oil

Ingredients | serves 4

- 4 garlic cloves, peeled
- 4oz (125g) fresh goat cheese (Chèvre or Montrachet, if possible), crumbled
- 1 tbsp thyme leaves, freshly picked (if possible)
- 4 x semiboneless quail, ribs and backbone removed (ask your butcher to do this for you)
- 4 chives, trimmed and divided into strips
- 1 tbsp vegetable oil, for frying
- salt and freshly ground black pepper

for the mango salsa
- 2 ripe mangoes, peeled, pitted, and diced into 1/2 in (1 cm) cubes
- 1/2 cucumber, seeded and diced (as above)
- 1 sweet red bell pepper (capsicum), seeded and diced (as above)
- 1 jalapeño chile (chilli), seeded and minced
- 2 scallions (spring onions), outer leaves removed, trimmed, and finely chopped
- 2 tbsp mint leaves, freshly picked (if possible) and finely chopped
- 1 tbsp cider vinegar
- 1 tbsp olive oil

Blackened garlic & goat cheese stuffed quail

1 To make the mango salsa, mix all the ingredients together in a large mixing bowl. Cover and set aside at room temperature for 1–1 1/2 hours before serving.

2 Preheat oven to 400°F (200°C/Gas Mark 6). Meanwhile, to make the filling for the quail, set a heavy cast-iron frying pan over medium-high heat. Place the garlic cloves in the pan. Let blacken over 65–70 percent of the surface, about 3 minutes, then remove from the pan.

3 Mince the blackened cloves and place in a bowl. Add the goat cheese and thyme, and mix together to form a filling.

4 Season the quail inside and out with salt and pepper. Transfer the filling to a pastry bag and pipe it into the seasoned cavity of each quail. Truss the legs of the quail together with strips of chives.

5 Set the frying pan over medium-high heat and add the vegetable oil. Place the quail in the skillet frying pan, breast side down, and fry for 2–2 1/2 minutes.

6 Turn the quail over and place the frying pan in the oven for 8–10 minutes, or until golden brown all over.

7 To serve, arrange the quail on serving plates and serve immediately, garnished with mango salsa.

Note_The salsa serves 4–6 people. Remember to allow enough time for the salsa to marinate (see Step 1). The salsa can be made in advance and stored, covered in the refrigerator, for up to 2 days. If you like, the quail may be served on a bed of arugula (rocket) leaves.

Garlic & red chile-rubbed rack of lamb with ancho & sun-dried cherry compote

Ingredients | serves 4

- 2 x 8-bone racks of lamb (ask your butcher to prepare them for you)
- roasted garlic mash (see page 46), to serve

for the garlic & red chile rub
- 4oz (125g) New Mexican red chile powder (available from spice stores and good supermarkets)
- 8 garlic cloves, peeled
- 2 tbsp rosemary leaves, freshly picked (if possible), chopped
- 2 tbsp olive oil
- 1½ tbsp sea salt

for the compote
- 1 large red onion, cut into fine strips
- 4 ancho chiles (chillies) (available from spice stores and good supermarkets), stemmed, seeded, and cut into ¼ in (5 mm) strips
- 4 oz (125g) sun-dried cranberries
- 2 lemons, rind removed and juiced
- ¾ cup (6oz/180g) sugar

1 Place all the ingredients for the rub into the bowl of a food processor and pulse until an even paste is formed, about 1 minute. Rub the lamb with the mixture to coat evenly, then refrigerate, covered, for at least 2 hours.

2 To make the compote, in a large, heavy saucepan, place the onion strips and then the chiles, cranberries, lemon rind, and juice, and finally the sugar. Do not stir the mixture.

3 Place the pan over a medium-low heat, stirring occasionally, until caramelized and syrupy, 20–25 minutes. (If the compote becomes too dry, add a scant ½ cup (4floz/125ml) water and cook for another 5 minutes.) Set aside.

4 To cook the lamb, preheat oven to 325°F (160°C/Gas Mark 3). Place the prepared lamb on a baking sheet and roast on the top rack of the oven for about 15 minutes for medium-rare meat, depending on size, or to taste. Remove and let rest for 3 minutes before carving. Slowly reheat the compote.

5 To serve, arrange the lamb on plates, drizzle the compote on the side, and serve immediately with some roasted garlic mashed potatoes.

Note_The lamb needs to be prepared and refrigerated, covered in plastic wrap, for 2 hours in advance of the main recipe.

Broiled Catalonia chorizo salad with Manchego cheese, garlic chips, arugula & black olives

1 | Preheat a broiler (grill), then cook the chorizo for 5 minutes on each side. Keep warm.

2 | To make the garlic chips, slice the garlic cloves so that they are paper thin, using a mandoline, if possible. In a large, heavy frying pan over low heat, heat the butter until hot, then add the sliced garlic. Fry until lightly browned, about 5 minutes. Remove from the pan with a slotted spoon and drain on paper towels.

3 | To make the salad, in a bowl, toss together the arugula, parsley, olives, and piquillo peppers. Dress with olive oil and vinegar, then season with freshly ground black pepper.

4 | To serve, place 2 chorizo in the center of each plate, together with the cheese and some salad. Garnish with garlic chips and serve immediately.

Ingredients | serves 4

- 8 small whole chorizo
- 2 bunches arugula (rocket), leaves picked
- 10 flat-leaf parsley leaves
- 15 Kalamata olives, pitted
- 4 Spanish piquillo peppers, drained and chopped (if unavailable, roast your own bell peppers/capsicums)
- 1/4 cup (2 fl oz/60 ml) extra virgin olive oil
- 2 tbsp red wine vinegar (preferably Cabernet Sauvignon)
- 3 oz (90 g) Manchego cheese, thinly sliced
- freshly ground black pepper

for the garlic chips

- 6 garlic cloves, peeled
- 2 cups (16 fl oz/500 ml) melted clarified butter (to make, place butter in a heavy saucepan over low heat and cook out until the fat separates; skim and strain)

for the Asian pear salad

_ 2 small, firm, and crunchy pears (preferably Asian/nashi), cored, then cut into quarters and sliced
_ 3 shiso leaves (if unavailable, substitute basil or cilantro /coriander), sliced
_ 1 scallion (spring onion), trimmed and cut on a bias
_ ¼ tsp ground coriander seeds
_ 1 tsp minced shallot
_ 2 tbsp canoli (rapeseed) oil
_ 1 tbsp rice wine vinegar
_ 1 lemongrass stalk, minced

Pan-seared foie gras on Asian pear salad with shiso & roasted garlic brioche

1| To make the salad, gently toss all the ingredients together in a bowl. Cover with plastic wrap and then leave to marinate at room temperature for 30 minutes.

2| Meanwhile, to make the brioche, preheat oven to 350°F (180°C/Gas Mark 4). Place the yeast in a small mixing bowl and pour the milk over the top. Leave for 5 minutes to allow the yeast to activate, then mix together to dissolve the yeast.

3| In the large bowl of a food processor, process to combine the remaining dry ingredients, about 5 minutes. Fit the hook attachment, then add the milk and eggs. Beat at low speed until a dough forms, about 10 minutes.

4| Add the roasted garlic flesh and butter. Continue to beat until the dough pulls away from the sides of the bowl. Knead until smooth and elastic.

5| Grease 6 x 3 in (7.5 cm) diameter brioche molds. Shape the dough into 6 balls and transfer to the molds. Leave for 40 minutes in a warm place to rise. Bake for 15–20 minutes until golden brown. Place on a cooling rack and set aside.

6| Heat a heavy frying pan over high heat, then season the foie gras. Sear 2 pieces at a time until golden brown, about 1 minute on each side. Transfer to paper towels.

7| To serve, place some pear salad in the center of each plate. Slice each brioche widthwise through the center and place on top of the salad. Add the seared foie gras and serve immediately.

Note _ Shiso is a Japanese leaf with a cinnamon and basil flavor.

Ingredients | serves 6

_ 6 x 2oz (60g) portions foie gras, veins removed
_ salt and freshly ground black pepper

for the roasted garlic brioche
_ 2 tsp active dry yeast
_ ¼ cup (2 fl oz/60 ml) milk, warmed
_ 2¼ cups (12oz/375g) all-purpose (plain) flour plus 3 tbsp
_ 2 tbsp superfine (caster) sugar
_ pinch of ground chipotle chile (chilli) (available from spice stores or substitute smoked paprika)
_ 1 tsp salt
_ 4 eggs
_ 12 roasted garlic cloves (place some rock salt in a large, heavy frying pan, top with a garlic bulb, and roast for 25 minutes at 350°F (180°C/Gas Mark 4). Slice the top from the bulb and squeeze the flesh out into a bowl)
_ ¼ cup (2oz/60g) unsalted butter, softened at room temperature, plus extra for greasing

Ingredients | serves 4

- 2 tbsp vegetable oil
- 1 lb (500 g) chicken carcass (or chicken wings), chopped
- 1 large onion, sliced
- 2 thumb-sized pieces ginger, peeled and chopped
- 8 large garlic cloves, peeled and crushed
- 2 red chiles (chillies), trimmed and seeded
- 5 cups (2 pints/1.2 liters) coconut milk
- 1 1/4 cups (1/2 pint/300 ml) water
- 2 lemongrass stalks, crushed
- 4 kaffir lime leaves, crushed
- 1 bunch cilantro (coriander), washed, then leaves picked and stems chopped
- 5 scallions (spring onions), trimmed (3 are roughly sliced and 2 are finely sliced for the garnish)
- 1 x 1 lb (500 g) package rice vermicelli noodles
- 2 chicken breasts, skinned, boned, and cut into 1/2 in (1 cm) dice
- 3 tbsp fish sauce
- juice of 1 lime
- salt and freshly ground black pepper

Spicy garlic chicken laksa

1 Heat a large, heavy pot and add the vegetable oil. Quickly brown the chicken carcass (or wings) over medium heat, letting the meat take on some color before stirring to evenly brown and allow a strong aroma of chicken to be released. (The caramelization is the first step to making a good soup.)

2 Reduce the heat and add the onion, ginger, garlic, and chiles. Cover and cook for 10 minutes over low heat, and then stir in the coconut milk and water. Cover and let simmer for about 20 minutes until the broth takes on a fragrant, fresh roast chicken aroma. If it has not, cook for another 10 minutes. (Remember, it is the aroma you are looking for and not the flavor at this point. Once you add seasoning to an already-aromatic broth, it is sure to taste good.)

3 Add the lemongrass, kaffir lime leaves, cilantro stems (reserve the leaves for the garnish) and 3 roughly sliced scallions. Cover and let simmer for about another 30 minutes. Turn off the heat and let stand, covered, for another 30 minutes to cool.

4 Soak the noodles in a saucepan of hot water for about 10 minutes.

5 Pour the soup through a large strainer (discard the bones and aromatic ingredients) into a second pot. Return to a low heat and bring just to the boiling point, then reduce the heat to a simmer again. (At this stage, the soup should have a depth and fresh, aromatic flavor. Do not boil too much or the flavor will become gray.)

6 Drain the noodles and add to the soup along with the diced chicken. Season with fish sauce, salt, and pepper. Add just enough lime juice to cut the sweetness of the coconut milk and let simmer, about 5 minutes.

7 | To serve, place equal amounts of noodles and chicken in each bowl and pour the soup over the top. Sprinkle with cilantro leaves and the reserved scallions. Serve immediately with chopsticks and large soup spoons.

Note_ When making this soup, the secret is not to let it boil for long periods. A bare simmer is perfect. Although it has a chicken base, fish and shellfish can also be added, if liked. With a smaller batch of laksa (just halve the quantity), you can easily make red chicken curry. Just add some Thai red curry paste at the same time as the onions. Allow a whole chicken breast per person (add to the soup when you reach Step 6, above) and serve with boiled jasmine rice. Jasmine rice is long-grain rice, popular in Southeast Asia. It is also known as Thai fragrant rice and is available in most good supermarkets and Asian food stores.

Chicken Kiev style with baby leeks & mashed potato

Ingredients | serves 4

_ 4 x 6oz (180g) chicken breasts, skin removed and filleted (ask your butcher to do this for you)
_ 4 x 8-in (20-cm) square spring roll wrappers (available in Asian stores and good supermarkets)
_ a little olive oil (optional)
_ about 2 cups (14oz/400g) mashed potato
_ 12 baby leeks, trimmed and outer leaves removed
_ ¼ cup (2oz/60g) butter, plus extra for brushing

for the garlic butter
_ 1 cup (8oz/250g) butter, softened at room temperature
_ 1 garlic clove, peeled and finely chopped
_ 1 shallot, finely chopped
_ 4 tsp finely chopped parsley
_ a little Pernod (optional)
_ salt and freshly ground black pepper

1 | Preheat oven to 400–425°F (200–220°C/Gas Mark 6–7). Meanwhile, to make the garlic butter, place the butter in the bowl of a food processor or blender. Beat until white. Stir in the garlic, shallot, and parsley, then season with salt and pepper. For extra flavor, add a little Pernod to taste.

2 | To prepare the Kiev, place the filleted chicken breasts between 2 layers of plastic wrap. Flatten them with a meat mallet to a thickness of about ⅛ in (3 mm).

3 | Spread the chicken breasts with the garlic butter and press the fillets together to join.

4 | On a work surface, spread out the sheets of spring roll wrappers. Brush with melted butter, then place a chicken breast in the center of each one. Fold the wrapper over to form triangular shapes, then press the edges together to secure.

5 | Grease a baking sheet with olive oil or butter and place the chicken parcels on top. Bake slowly in the oven (keep checking) until the butter inside the wrappers has melted and the chicken is cooked through and slightly firm, 8–10 minutes. Meanwhile, reheat the mashed potato and quickly soften the baby leeks in plenty of boiling salted water, about 2 minutes. Finish by sautéing in butter, about 1 minute.

6 | To serve, place a chicken parcel on each plate and garnish with mashed potatoes and baby leeks. Serve immediately.

Note_The garlic butter can be made a few days in advance. To store, place in a sealed container and refrigerate. To prepare the leeks in advance, cook as above, then plunge straight into iced water to arrest the cooking process. Drain and store, covered in a bowl in the refrigerator, for up to 2 days. If you are cooking the Kiev parcels for just 1–2 people, heat a heavy, nonstick frying pan, add some clarified butter, and fry for about 2 minutes until brown and crispy. Bake in the oven as above for 7–8 minutes.

glossary

Aioli_is a rich garlic mayonnaise, ideally suited for use with various soups, fish, egg and vegetable dishes. It is known as "Alioli" in Spain.

Arugula_is also known as rucola, rughetta, roquette, and rocket, and is a peppery salad leaf plant. Although leaf sizes vary, the more mature and larger leaves indicate that the taste will be better and stronger. Rucola di Capri, a wild rocket with very small leaves, is more like a herb than a salad plant. Once picked, arugula should be used as soon as possible. Wash it well and carefully remove any yellowed leaves and tough stems.

Borlotti beans_are speckled red and white when fresh (from about September through to mid-January), and they turn pink as soon as they begin to cook. They are similar to cannellini beans but rougher in texture and more starchy.

Carta di Musica_is a traditional Sardinian bread, also known as pane carasau, and made without yeast. It has a crisp, paper-thin texture, resembling the thin parchment used classically for writing music, and is golden in color. Cooked in large rounds on a baker's slab, it keeps well over long periods. Armenian cracker bread (lahvosh) may be substituted.

Chipotle peppers_are a smoked variety of jalapeño peppers.

Empanaditas_are Mexican potato pancakes which may be filled with meat or vegetable mixes. They are then baked in the oven and served with a fresh tomato sauce.

Escalivada_is a Catalonian dish of roasted vegetables that takes its name from the verb "escalivar", meaning to cook in hot ashes. It is ideal for the barbecue but equally delicious when cooked in a conventional oven.

New season's garlic_is the very moist, thinly skinned variety of garlic that is available in the late spring and early summer. It is sometimes referred to as "wet garlic".

Orecchiette_A pasta originating in the Apulia region of Italy. The word translates as "little ears", referring to the small, husklike shape of the noodles.

Pan Amb Tomat_This is a traditional Spanish breakfast dish: quite simply a piece of good bread drizzled with olive oil, rubbed with a clove of garlic and then with a very ripe tomato.

Pennette_A smalller version of penne.

Shisu_A Japanese leaf with a flavor similar to basil or cinnamon.

Skordalia_is a Greek garlic sauce of a mayonnaise consistency that varies from region to region. It is made up of boiled potatoes mashed with lemon juice and olive oil and often contains ground almonds and raw garlic, although roasted garlic may be used for a subtler flavor.

Sumac_A North African spice.

Wild garlic_ grows in the country and is readily available in the spring. Only the dark green broad leaves heavily scented with the smell of garlic are eaten. The bulb itself is far too tough.

contributors

Michael McEnearney
THE PHARMACY
_ Corn soup
_ Roast chicken with fresh borlotti beans & aioli
_ Roast leg of lamb with Provençal vegetables & skordalia

Rocky Durham
SANTA FE
_ Roasted garlic empanaditas with blackened tomato chipotle sauce
_ Blackened garlic & goat cheese stuffed quail
_ Garlic & red chile-rubbed rack of lamb with ancho & sun-dried cherry compote

Pascal Proyart
RESTAURANT 101
_ Sardines filled with pesto potatoes & tomato salsa
_ Brandade of cod with garlic bruschetta
_ Chicken Kiev style with baby leeks & mashed potato

Alastair Little
ALASTAIR LITTLE
_ Grilled eggplant with garlic & anchovy dip
_ Roast new season's garlic with homemade cheese
_ Baked garlic soup with a poached egg

Sue Lewis
LOMO
_ Pan amb tomat
_ Alioli (with patatas alioli, deep-fried squid and zucchini fritters)
_ Escalivada
_ Chicken, chorizo & vegetable paella
_ Roasted red bell pepper & garlic soup with goat cheese & garlic toast

Ray Brown
BALI SUGAR
_ Pan-seared foie gras on Asian pear salad with shiso & roasted garlic brioche
_ Broiled Catalonia chorizo salad with Manchego cheese, garlic chips, arugula & black olives

Fabio Trabocchi
FLORIANA
_ White garlic soup with langoustines & almond-infused mushrooms
_ Squab with sweet garlic
_ Crudités with pesto of garlic, chervil & fennel

Eric Chavot
THE CAPITAL
_ Smoked haddock with aioli potatoes & garlic chips
_ Pan-seared scallops with garlic purée & deep-fried parsley
_ Garlic & onion velouté

Chris Galvin
ORRERY
_ Goat cheese & chard cannelloni with garlic & rosemary sabayon
_ Gratin of caramelized Belgian endives, smoked garlic & Comté cheese
_ Tagine of lobster with couscous & garlic confit

Cass Titcombe
THE COLLECTION
_ Seared salt-cured salmon with porcini crust & celeriac & garlic purée
_ Pennette with wild garlic, pine nuts, broccoli & Parmesan
_ Roast lamb with roast garlic & rosemary potatoes

Chris Benians
STRADA
_ Wild garlic risotto
_ Bagna cauda
_ Penne with roasted garlic pesto

Tim Tolley
VONG
_ Monkfish studded with young garlic, saffron tagliatelle & fennel sauce
_ Steamed skate with wild garlic & oyster mushrooms

Dean Peck
LIVEBAIT
_ Pan-Asian oysters Rockefeller
_ Shrimp wonton with spicy sweet & sour sauce & Hawaiian salsa
_ Black mussels with Thai red curry broth

Terry Stewart
PASHA
_ Shrimp chermoula
_ Spiced raw tuna with Moroccan tabbouleh
_ Broiled rib-eye steak with tomato, eggplant & chickpeas garnished with zaatar

Lee Purcell
SARTORIA
_ Roasted garlic & bread soup
_ Roasted garlic, tomatoes, olives, anchovies & crisp bread
_ Chicken baked in sea salt with garlic

Mark Read
BAM-BOU
_ Crispy squid with bitter lemon
_ Monkfish with turmeric, dill & onion
_ Sesame lamb and shiitake sauté with mint & shallots

Simon Fennick
SUGAR CLUB
_ Salmon ceviche
_ Spicy garlic chicken laksa

Ken Whitehead
LANGANS BRASSERIE
_ Grilled pita bread filled with lamb, garlic & thyme
_ Potato & goat cheese soup with garlic leaves

Maddalena Bonino
MASH
_ Risotto with mussels, garlic, squid & shrimp

Richard Sawyer
ATLANTIC
_ Garlic baked plum tomatoes with lemon
  thyme, parsley & wilted arugula
_ Orecchiette with vine-ripened cherry tomatoes & chorizo
_ Roasted sweet butternut squash risotto with new season's garlic & cilantro

index

Aioli (Alioli) 36, 153
   Aioli potatoes 96-7
   Roast chicken with fresh borlotti beans & aioli 139
anchovies:
   Bagna cauda 27
   Garlic and anchovy dip 28
   Roasted garlic, tomatoes, olives, anchovies & crisp bread 54
arugula 153
   Broiled Catalonia chorizo salad with Monchego cheese, garlic chips, arugula & black olives 145
   Garlic-baked plum tomatoes with lemon thyme, parsley & wilted arugula 42
aubergines see eggplants

Bagna cauda 27
beef: Broiled rib-eye steak with tomato, eggplant & chickpeas garnished with zaatar 132
Beets, Roasted 122-3
bell peppers see peppers (bell)
borlotti beans 153
   Roast chicken with fresh borlotti beans & aioli 139
Brandade of cod with garlic bruschetta 114
bread:
   Brandade of cod with garlic bruschetta 114
   Garlic toast 18
   Pan amb tomat 38
   Roasted garlic & bread soup 21
broccoli: Pennette with wild garlic, pine nuts, broccoli & Parmesan 68
bruschetta: Brandade of cod with garlic bruschetta 114
bulgur wheat: Spiced raw tuna with Moroccan tabbouleh 94
Butter, Garlic 150

celeriac: Seared salt-cured salmon with porcini crust & celeriac & garlic purée 78
chard: Goat cheese & chard cannelloni with garlic & rosemary sabayon 58-9
cheese:
   Blackened garlic & goat cheese stuffed quail 140
   Broiled Catalonia chorizo salad with Monchego cheese, garlic chips, arugula & black olives 145
   Goat cheese & chard cannelloni with garlic & rosemary sabayon 58-9
   Gratin of caramelized Belgian endives, smoked garlic & Comté cheese 53
   Pennette with wild garlic, pine nuts, broccoli & Parmesan 68
   Potato & goat cheese soup with garlic leaves 12
   Roast new season's garlic with homemade cheese 35
   Roasted red bell pepper & garlic soup with goat cheese & garlic toast 18
chervil: Crudités with pesto of garlic, chervil & fennel 31
chicken:
   Chicken baked in sea salt with garlic 122-3
   Chicken, chorizo & vegetable paella 70
   Chicken Kiev style with baby leeks & mashed potato 150
   Roast chicken with fresh borlotti beans & aioli 139
   Spicy garlic chicken laksa 148-9
chickpeas: Broiled rib-eye steak with tomato, eggplant & chickpeas garnished with zaatar 132
chicory see endive
chiles (chillies): Garlic & red chile-rubbed rack of lamb with ancho & sun-dried cherry compote 142
chorizo:
   Broiled Catalonia chorizo salad with Monchego cheese, garlic chips, arugula & black olives 145
   Chicken, chorizo & vegetable paella 70
   Orecchiette with vine-ripened cherry tomatoes & chorizo 64
cilantro: Roasted sweet butternut squash risotto with new season's garlic & cilantro 63
Coconut cream 32
cod: Brandade of cod with garlic bruschetta 114
Corn soup 16
courgettes see zucchini
couscous: Tagine of lobster with couscous & garlic confit 112-13
cranberries: Ancho & sun-dried cherry compote 142
crisp bread: Roasted garlic, tomatoes, olives, anchovies & 54
Crudités with pesto of garlic, chervil & fennel 31

dill: Monkfish with turmeric, dill & onion 81
dips:
   Alioli 36
   Bagna cauda 27
   Garlic and anchovy dip 28
   Pesto dip 31
dressing, Ginger & garlic 86

eggplants:
   Broiled rib-eye steak with tomato, eggplant & chickpeas garnished with zaatar 132
   Escalivada 50
   Grilled eggplants with garlic & anchovy dip 28
   Roast leg of lamb with Provençal vegetables & skordalia 136-7
   Shrimp chermoula 102
eggs:
   Alioli 36
   Baked garlic soup with a poached egg 15
elephant garlic 8
empanaditas 153
   Roasted garlic empanaditas with blackened tomato chipotle sauce 46-7
endives: Gratin of caramelized Belgian endives, smoked garlic & Comté cheese 53
Escalivada 50, 153

fennel:
   Crudités with pesto of garlic, chervil & fennel 31
   Monkfish studded with young garlic, saffron tagliatelle & fennel sauce 106-7
foie gras: Pan-seared foie gras on Asian pear salad with shiso & roasted garlic brioche 147

garlic:
   cooking time 9
   culinary uses 9
   minerals in 8
   preparation 9
   storage 8
   types 6-8
   wild 153
garlic chives 8
Ginger & garlic dressing 86
glossary 153

Gratin of caramelized Belgian endives, smoked garlic & Comté cheese 53
haddock: Smoked haddock with aioli potatoes & garlic chips 96-7
Herb topping 32
Horseradish sauce 123

lamb:
   Garlic & red chile-rubbed rack of lamb with ancho & sun-dried cherry compote 142
   Grilled pita bread filled with lamb, garlic & thyme 120
   Roast lamb with roast garlic & rosemary potatoes 128-9
   Roast leg of lamb with Provençal vegetables & skordalia 136-7
   Sesame lamb & shiitake sauté with mint & shallots 119
langoustines: White garlic soup with langoustines & almond-infused mushrooms 22
leeks: Chicken Kiev style with baby leeks & mashed potato 150
lobster: Tagine of lobster with couscous & garlic confit 112-13

mango:
   Hawaiian salsa 93
   Mango salsa 140
minerals 8
monkfish:
   Monkfish studded with young garlic, saffron tagliatelle & fennel sauce 106-7
   Monkfish with turmeric, dill & onion 81
mushrooms:
   Seared salt-cured salmon with porcini crust & celeriac & garlic purée 78
   Sesame lamb & shiitake sauté with mint & shallots 119
   Steamed skate with wild garlic & oyster mushrooms 100-1
   White garlic soup with langoustines & almond-infused mushrooms 22
mussels:
   Black mussels with Thai red curry broth 108
   Risotto with mussels, garlic, squid & shrimp 74

olives:
   Broiled Catalonia chorizo salad

with Monchego cheese, garlic chips, arugula & black olives 145
Roasted garlic, tomatoes, olives, anchovies & crisp bread 54

onions:
- Escalivada 50
- Garlic and onion velouté 45
- Monkfish with turmeric, dill & onion 81

orecchiette 153
- Orecchiette with vine-ripened cherry tomatoes & chorizo 64

oysters: Pan-Asian oysters Rockefeller 32-3

paella: Chicken, chorizo & vegetable paella 70
Pan amb tomat 38, 153
Pan-Asian oysters Rockefeller 32-3

parsley:
- Garlic-baked plum tomatoes with lemon thyme, parsley & wilted arugula 42
- Moroccan tabbouleh 94
- Pan-seared scallops with garlic purée & deep-fried parsley 89
- Roasted garlic pesto 73

pasta dishes:
- Garlic and onion velouté 45
- Goat cheese & chard cannelloni with garlic & rosemary sabayon 58-9
- Monkfish studded with young garlic, saffron tagliatelle & fennel sauce 106-7
- Orecchiette with vine-ripened cherry tomatoes & chorizo 64
- Penne with roasted garlic pesto 73
- Pennette with wild garlic, pine nuts, broccoli & Parmesan 68

Patatas alioli 36
pears: Pan-seared foie gras on Asian pear salad with shiso & roasted garlic brioche 147
Penne with roasted garlic pesto 73
pennette 153
- Pennette with wild garlic, pine nuts, broccoli & Parmesan 68

peppers (bell):
- Escalivada 50
- Mango salsa 140
- Roast leg of lamb with Provençal vegetables & skordalia 136-7
- Roasted red bell pepper & garlic soup with goat cheese & garlic toast 18

pesto:
- Pesto of garlic, chervil & fennel 31
- Pesto potatoes 82-3
- Pesto sauce 68
- Roasted garlic pesto 73

pigeon: Squab with sweet garlic 126

pine nuts:
- Pennette with wild garlic, pine nuts, broccoli & Parmesan 68
- Pesto potatoes 82-3

pita bread: Grilled pita bread filled with lamb, garlic & thyme 120

potatoes:
- Chicken Kiev style with baby leeks & mashed potato 150
- Escalivada 50
- Patatas alioli 36
- Potato & goat cheese soup with garlic leaves 12
- Roast lamb with roast garlic & rosemary potatoes 128-9
- Sardines filled with pesto potatoes & tomato salsa 82-3
- Skordalia 136-7
- Smoked haddock with aioli potatoes & garlic chips 96-7

quail: Blackened garlic & goat cheese stuffed quail 140

ramsons 8

rice:
- Chicken, chorizo & vegetable paella 70
- Risotto with mussels, garlic, squid & shrimp 74
- Roasted sweet butternut squash risotto with new season's garlic & cilantro 63
- Wild garlic risotto 67

rosemary:
- Garlic & rosemary potatoes 128-9
- Goat cheese & chard cannelloni with garlic & rosemary sabayon 58-9

salmon:
- Salmon ceviche 86
- Seared salt-cured salmon with porcini crust & celeriac & garlic purée 78

salsa:
- Hawaiian salsa 93
- Mango salsa 140
- Salsa verde 122
- Tomato salsa 82-3

Sardines filled with pesto potatoes & tomato salsa 82-3

sauces:
- Alioli 36
- Fennel sauce 106-7
- Horseradish sauce 123
- Spicy sweet & sour sauce 92-3

scallops: Pan-seared scallops with garlic purée & deep-fried parsley 89

Sesame lamb & shiitake sauté with mint & shallots 119

shrimp:
- Risotto with mussels, garlic, squid & shrimp 74
- Shrimp chermoula 102
- Shrimp wantons with spicy sweet & sour sauce & Hawaiian salsa 92-3

skate: Steamed skate with wild garlic & oyster mushrooms 100-1

skordalia 153
- Roast leg of lamb with Provençal vegetables & skordalia 136-7

Smoked haddock with aioli potatoes & garlic chips 96-7

soups:
- Baked garlic soup with a poached egg 15
- Corn soup 16
- Potato & goat cheese soup with garlic leaves 12
- Roasted garlic & bread soup 21
- Roasted red bell pepper & garlic soup with goat cheese & garlic toast 18
- Spicy garlic chicken laksa 148-9
- White garlic soup with langoustines & almond-infused mushrooms 22

Spiced raw tuna with Moroccan tabbouleh 94
Spicy garlic chicken laksa 148-9
Spicy sweet & sour sauce 92-3
spinach: Pan-Asian oysters Rockefeller 32-3
Squab with sweet garlic 126
squash: Roasted sweet butternut squash risotto with new season's garlic & cilantro 63

squid:
- Crispy squid with bitter lemon 90
- Deep-fried squid 36
- Risotto with mussels, garlic, squid & shrimp 74

steak: Broiled rib-eye steak with tomato, eggplant & chickpeas garnished with zaatar 132
storage 8
Sweet & sour sauce, Spicy 92-3

Swiss chard: Goat cheese & chard cannelloni with garlic & rosemary sabayon 58-9

tabbouleh: Spiced raw tuna with Moroccan tabbouleh 94
Tagine of lobster with couscous & garlic confit 112-13

thyme:
- Garlic-baked plum tomatoes with lemon thyme, parsley & wilted arugula 42
- Grilled pita bread filled with lamb, garlic & thyme 120

Toast, Garlic 18

tomatoes:
- Broiled rib-eye steak with tomato, eggplant & chickpeas garnished with zaatar 132
- Garlic-baked plum tomatoes with lemon thyme, parsley & wilted arugula 42
- Orecchiette with vine-ripened cherry tomatoes & chorizo 64
- Pan amb tomat 38
- Roast leg of lamb with Provençal vegetables & skordalia 136-7
- Roasted garlic empanaditas with blackened tomato chipotle sauce 46-7
- Roasted garlic, tomatoes, olives, anchovies & crisp bread 54
- Sardines filled with pesto potatoes & tomato salsa 82-3
- Shrimp chermoula 102

tuna: Spiced raw tuna with Moroccan tabbouleh 94

White garlic soup with langoustines & almond-infused mushrooms 22

wild garlic 153
- Wild garlic risotto 67

zaatar: Broiled rib-eye steak with tomato, eggplant & chickpeas garnished with zaatar 132

zucchini:
- Escalivada 50
- Zucchini fritters 36

acknowledgments

The publishers would like to thank all those restaurants and chefs who contributed their time and skills to the production of this book.

The chefs:
Claudio Aprile, Chris Benians, Maddalena Bonino, Eric Chavot, Rocky Durham, Sue Lewis, Alastair Little, Simon Fennick, Chris Galvin, Michael McEnearney, Dean Peck, Pascal Proyart, Lee Purcell, Mark Read, Richard Sawyer, Terry Stewart, Cass Titcombe, Tim Tolley, Fabio Trabocchi, and Ken Whitehead.

Thanks also to Andy Cameron, Sophie Broadbridge, Jane Donovan, Catherine Hawkins, and Gwynn-fyl Lowe.